CW00549205

SAMPLER & ANTIQUE NEEDLEWORK

A Year in Stitches—Volume II

Symbol of Excellence Publishers

Sampler & Antique Needlework: A Year in Stitches
Volume II

Copyright 1995 by Symbol of Excellence Publishers
405 Riverhills Business Park
Birmingham, AL 35242
USA

Published by Symbol of Excellence Publishers
A Division of PJS Publications, Inc.
A K ▶ III Communications Company

All rights reserved. No part of this book may be reproduced in any form or by any means without the prior written permission of the publisher, excepting brief quotations in connection with reviews written specifically for inclusion in a magazine or newspaper.

ISBN: 0-932437-04-4
Manufactured in the United States of America

Editor-in-Chief: Phyllis Hoffman

Executive Editor: Barbara Cockerham

Editor: Diane Kennedy-Jackson

Editorial Assistant: Susan Branch

Production Director: Perry James

Creative Director: Mac Jamieson

Executive Art Director: Yukie McLean

Art Director: Michael Whisenant

Graphic Designers: Dottie Barton, Scott Begley

Photographer: David L. Maxwell

Photography Stylist: Mike J. Jones

INTRODUCTION

*N*eedlework, especially samplermaking, carries with it a rich and fascinating past. Throughout the pages of recorded history, we read about the extraordinary needleworking skills of stitchers—from the most lowly of commoners to royalty of the highest order.

While some of the needlework from days gone by was used in a decorative manner, samplers were traditionally employed as teaching and reference pieces, upon which young girls practiced and perfected their abilities with needle and thread. On assorted ground cloths, young girls mastered the needleworking techniques that would afford them the necessary abilities with which to make, mend, and tend the linens and clothing of a household.

Needleworkers of modern times, by comparison, stitch generally for pleasure. But while our reasons for stitching have, with the passage of time, evolved very differently from those of our sister stitchers, we continue to share with these kindred spirits a place in needleworking history. Our affinity for the pieces of the past, combined with the creations we leave for future generations, will contribute to a centuries-old samplermaking tradition that has endured the test of time.

CONTENTS

Introduction 3

Historical Perspectives

Masterworks

Stitches in Time 8

Sarah Laker Sampler

*T*he Sarah Laker Sampler, *dated 1780, appears at first glance to be in remarkably good condition. Although a great deal of fading from exposure to light has occurred, as well as damage around the edges from the board and nails that were used to mount it, the ground cloth shows little damage. Acquired in Yorktown, Virginia, this sampler includes the name of the stitcher's instructress, Elizabeth Gilbert.*

This colorful reproduction of the *Sarah Laker Sampler* features an unusual strawberry motif that may have been inspired by work from the 1600s. References to similar motifs from this period appear in a number of researchers' findings. The sawtooth pattern that forms the border was commonly used as a dividing band. The pair of deer enhances the uniqueness of this piece. Both animals include spots, which would indicate a fawn, but the deer on the right boasts antlers, which suggest an adult. The deer on the left is roughly the same size, but is without antlers. Was this an attempt to portray a stag and a doe? As the needlewoman of today works the stitches to create this delightful sampler, she may ponder this question, as well as the life of Sarah, a stitcher from the past.

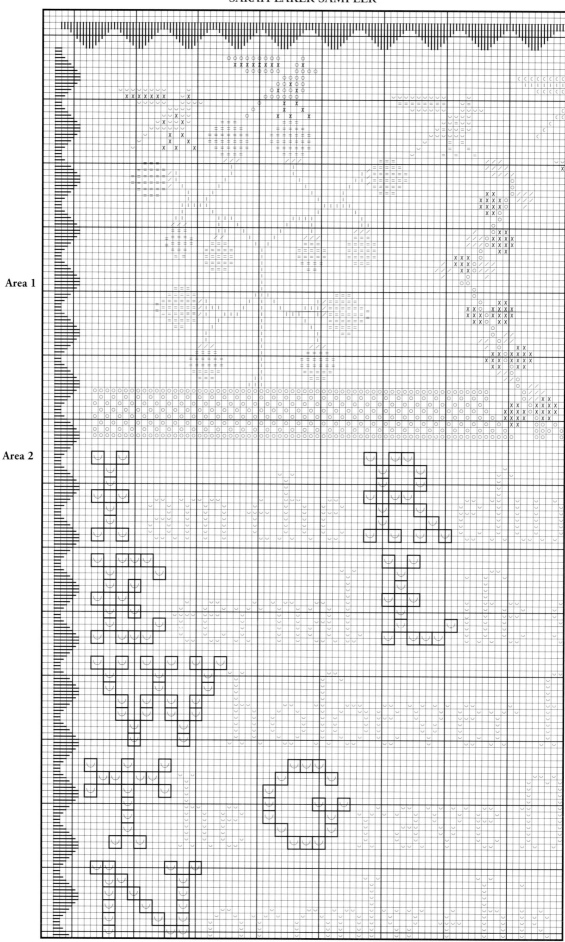

Area 1

Area 2

11

Shaded portion indicates overlap from previous page.

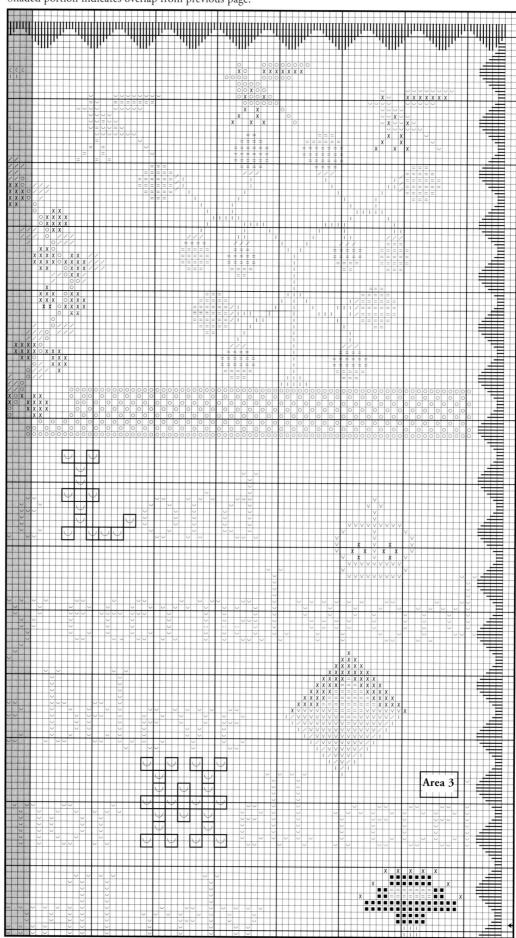

Area 3

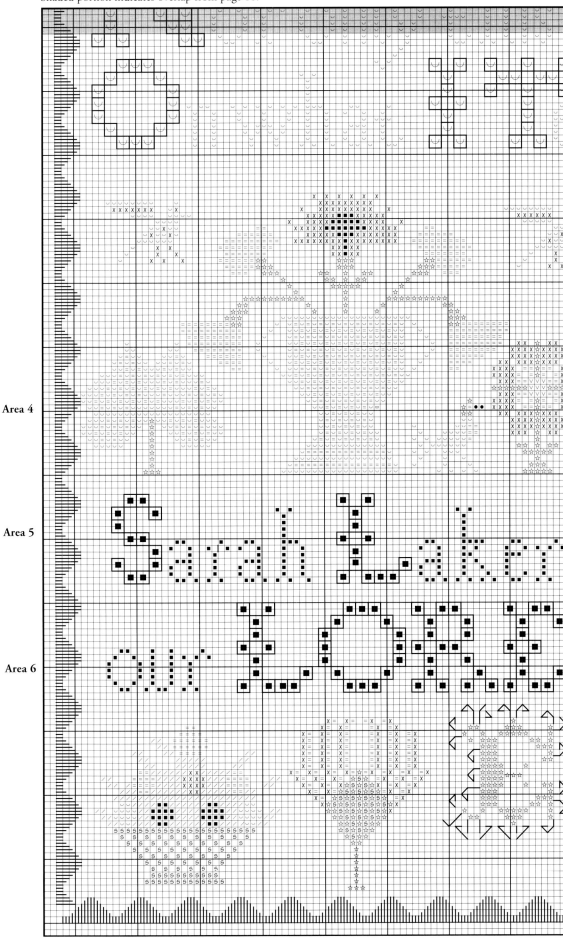

Area 4

Area 5

Area 6

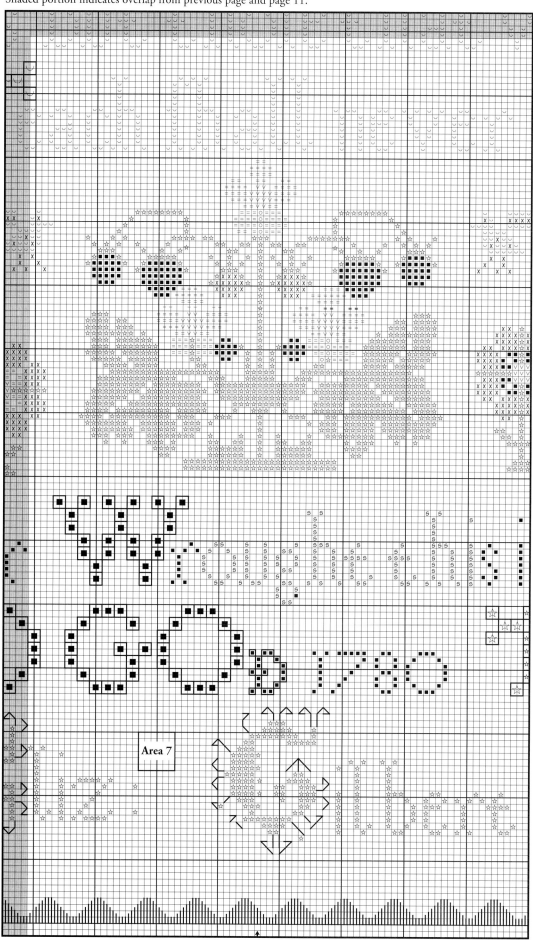

Area 7

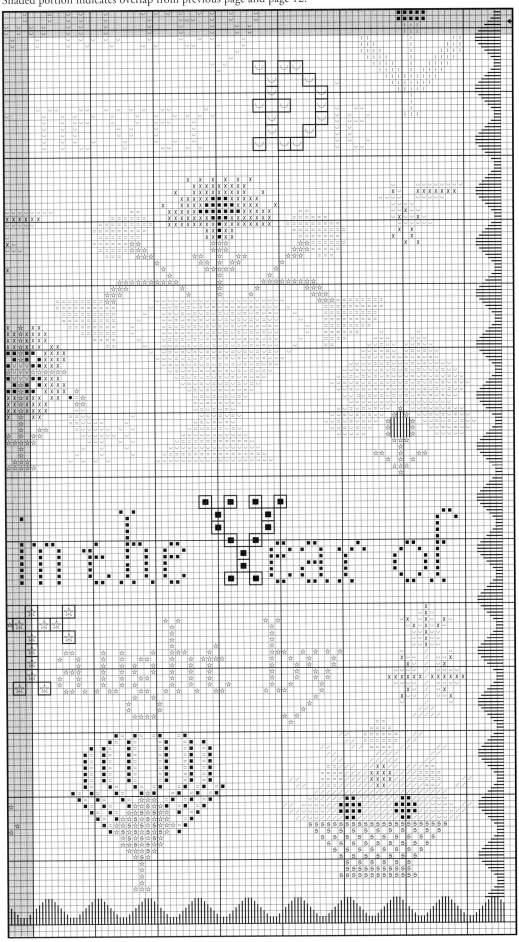

15

Sarah Laker Sampler

Kreinik Soie d'Alger	DMC	DMC FT	
X 2924	816	2346	garnet
■ 2925	815	2815	garnet, med.
ᴜ 1743	928	2928	gray-green, lt.
ᴄ 1442	827	2827	blue, vy. lt.
ı 526	830	2829	olive, dk.
● 4136	3371	2371	black-brown
╱ 2113	772	2472	pine green, lt.
○ 2216	730	2730	olive, vy. dk.
☆ 3424	523	—	fern green, lt.
ꙅ 4243	436	2436	tan
ᴠ 521	727	2727	topaz, vy. lt.
= 3711	822	2644	beige-gray, lt.

Fabric: 36-count cream Edinborough linen from Zweigart®
Stitch count: 282H x 239W
Design size:

25-count	22½" x 19⅛"
28-count	20⅛" x 17"
32-count	17⅝" x 15"
36-count	15⅝" x 13¼"

NOTE: This sampler includes displaced cross stitch. When symbol is placed over a line, the stitch should be placed in that position and worked over two threads.

Instructions: Cross stitch over two threads, using one strand of silk. Backstitch using one strand of silk.

Backstitch instructions:

3424 523 — filigree at bottom of sampler

3711 822 2644 eye of deer to left of tree

2925 815 2815 *r* in *Sarah*

Special instructions:

Border: Work satin stitch using one strand 521/727/2727, stitching in direction indicated by lines on chart.

Area 1: Cross stitch using 4136/3371/2371 where symbol ꙅ appears on deer to right of tree, and then repeat using 4243/436/2436.

Areas 2 & 5: Work Algerian eye stitch for capital letters, using one strand of silk.

Areas 3 & 7: Cross stitch over one thread, using one strand of silk.

Area 4: Work satin stitch in flower, using one strand 521/727/2727.

Area 6: Work Algerian eye stitch for *D* in *GOD* over two threads, using one strand of silk.

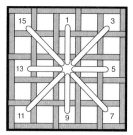

Algerian Eye Stitch

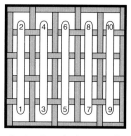

Satin Stitch (Vertical)

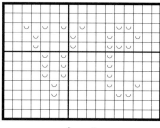

Area 3

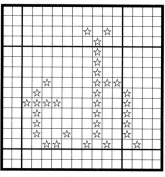

Area 7

History of Perforated Paper

One's hands simply could not be idle during the mid-nineteenth century. Propriety and etiquette were society's mainstays during the reign of Queen Victoria of England, and ladies spent their leisure hours engaged in many popular varieties of needlework.

The most widespread craze of those years was Berlin work, also called Berlin wool-work. With this colorful stitchery, ladies embellished practically every possible household item, including suspenders and slippers for beaux or husbands. One of the offshoots of the Berlin-work fad was stitching on perforated paper. This "paper" was more like perforated cardboard, also known as "Bristol board," with evenly spaced openings through which to stitch.

At first, ladies used their smaller Berlin-work patterns on perforated paper, stitching with Berlin wools and silks. They worked the patterns on greeting cards, needlecases and, especially, bookmarks. The minute size and simplicity of bookmarks made them an ideal ground for perforated-paper stitchery, which was easily mounted on brocade ribbon after the design was completed.[1] As interest grew, patternmakers began creating small bookmark designs, such as crosses, anchors, and short mottoes expressing that time period's moral and religious convictions (e.g., 'Holy Bible,' 'Temperance').[2]

As the Victorians began to embrace the lavish and ornate in every aspect of life during the third quarter of the nineteenth century, so the scale of perforated-paper projects increased from bookmarks to larger items such as sewing boxes and samplers (see our reproduction of the

Noble-Dog Sampler on page 18, the original of which measured 5⅞" x 10"), and further increased to very large mottoes that were simply framed and hung above door frames or on walls. Again, Biblical and moral mottoes were the prevalent designs used.

Perforated paper's vast appeal grew out of several of its positive characteristics. The perforated background did not need to be covered with wool, making projects less costly and less time-consuming. Perforated cards with pre-printed patterns were readily available and quite inexpensive, with advertised prices as low as one cent. And perhaps the biggest attraction to the stitchery was the simplicity of the technique— simple diagonal and cross stitches were the most common stitches. The only disadvantage of working with perforated paper was the threat of ripping the paper with a too-large needle, but the thicker the board was, the slimmer the chances of damaging it became.[3]

During the last quarter of the nineteenth century, "perforated work slipped from the parlor to the drawing room, and finally to the work room and kitchen. Later, perforated work could be found in farmhouses but not in townhouses, boarding-houses but not private residences."[4] The mania for perforated-paper mottoes struggled through the late 1870s, and by the early 1880s the pieces were denigrated in decorating manuals and entirely omitted from the middle-class needlework magazines whose pages they had once filled.

EDITOR'S NOTE
Today perforated paper is often used for stitching bookmarks, as it was in times past, and also appears as the ground used for a wide variety of modern-day stitchery projects, including beadwork.

ENDNOTES
[1]Barbara Morris, *Victorian Embroidery* (New York: Thomas Nelson & Sons, 1962), 172.

[2]Margaret Vincent, *The Ladies' Work Table: Domestic Needlework in Nineteenth-Century America* (Allentown: Allentown Art Museum, 1988), 37.

[3]Vincent, 39 & 57.

[4]Vincent, 81.

BIBLIOGRAPHY
Bath, Virginia Churchill. *Needlework in America.* New York: Viking Press, 1979.

Morris, Barbara. *Victorian Embroidery.* New York: Thomas Nelson & Sons, 1962.

Vincent, Margaret. *The Ladies' Work Table: Domestic Needlework in Nineteenth-Century America.* Allentown: Allentown Art Museum, 1988.

Noble-Dog Sampler

This charming design, a faithful reproduction of the *Noble-Dog Sampler,* features a host of bright floss colors. The antique has sustained a significant amount of water and light damage. The water damage on the front of the piece could be seen easily, but it was not until the sampler was removed from its frame that the extent of the light damage became apparent. The front of the antique, which has faded to assorted shades of brown, tan, and green, barely hinted at the impact of the vivid colors used to create it. On the back of the piece, the true colors chosen by the stitcher were revealed. Who would have imagined the existence of a bright-purple dog or a salmon- or lavender-colored deer? We can only guess at the age and name of the stitcher, who left only the initials *M G* for identification; but we assume that she

Antique—Front

Antique—Back

was fairly young. After all, an older child would know that a purple dog would be very rare indeed, and would probably be far too inhibited to stitch a motif such as a dog or a deer using a floss color that did not accurately depict the true-to-life color of the animal being stitched!

*T*he Noble-Dog Sampler, *while undated, was probably created sometime around the middle of the nineteenth century. At first glance, this sampler, which was worked on perforated paper, appears to be rather plain. Upon closer inspection, however, one notices the delightful verse, an ode, of sorts, to man's best friend.*

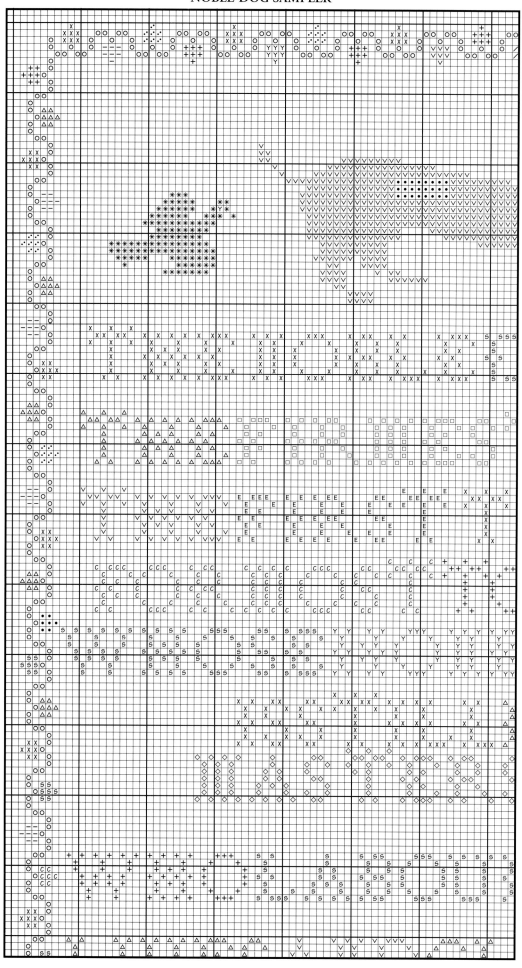

Shaded portion indicates overlap from previous page.

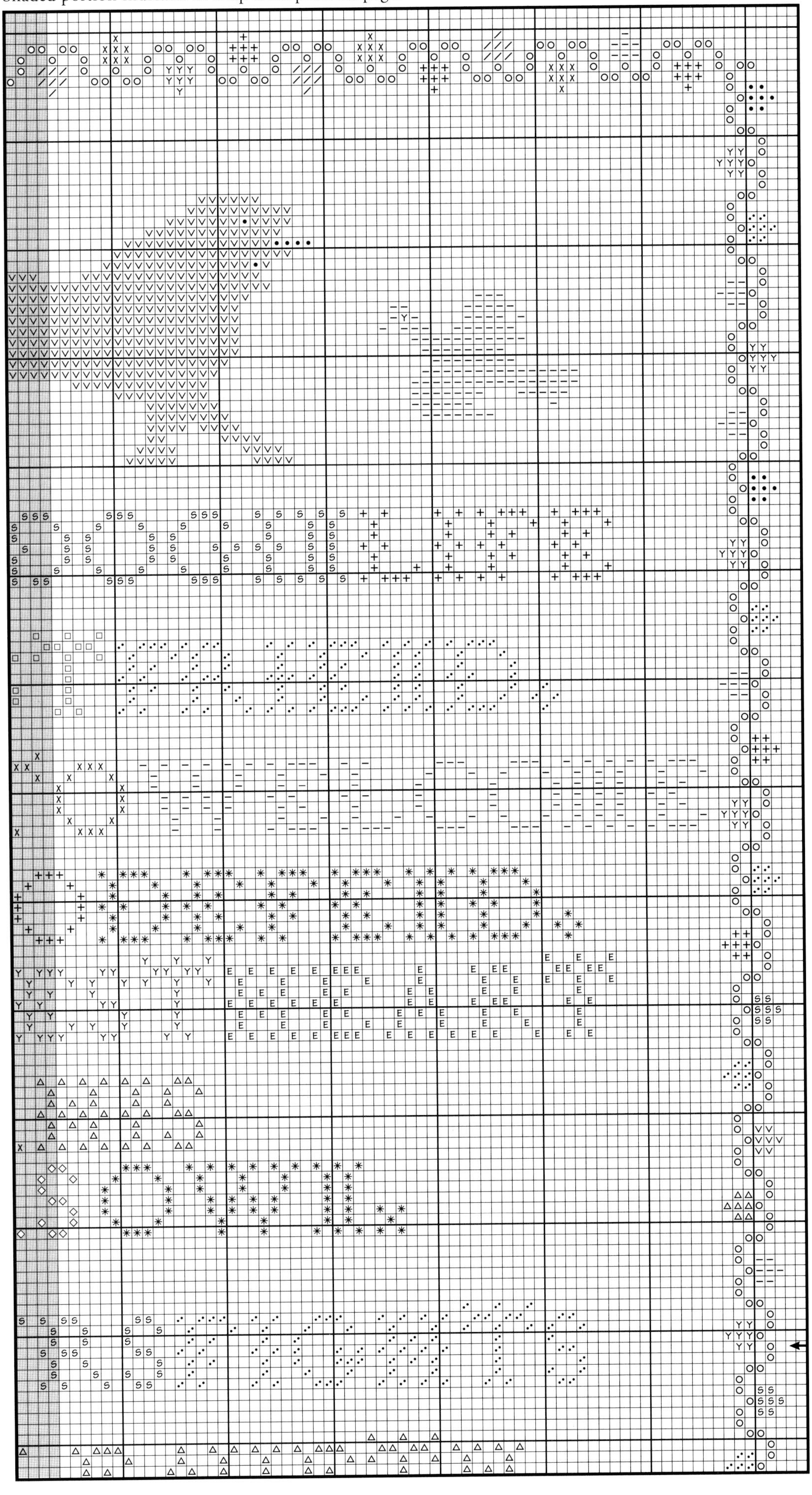

Shaded portion indicates overlap from page 20.

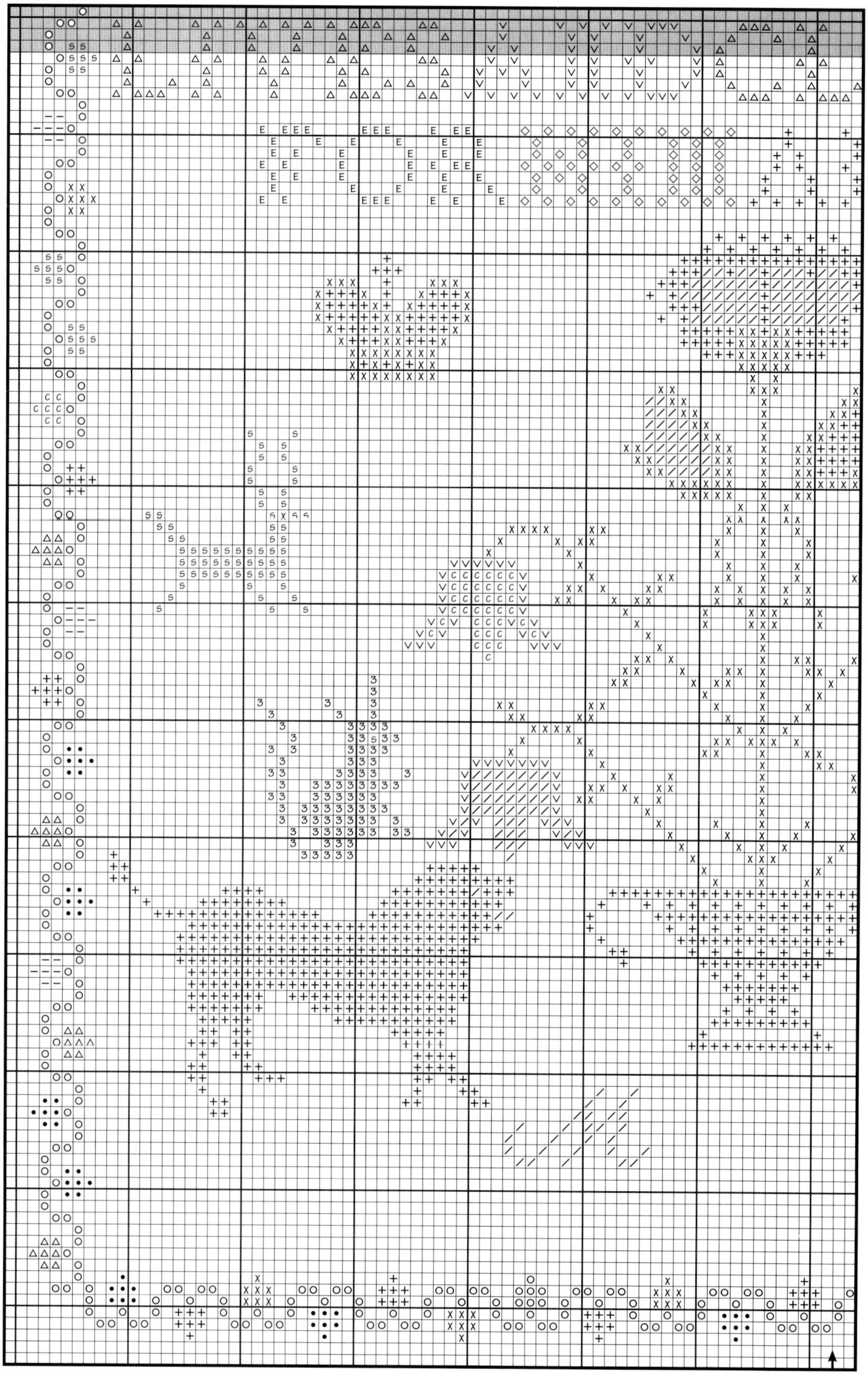

Noble-Dog Sampler

Kreinik

Soie d'Alger	DMC	FT				
X	1845	319	2319	pistachio, vy. dk.
○	4246	680	2782	old gold, dk.

	Soie d'Alger	DMC	FT	
+	4635	315	2315	mauve, dk.
✳	4136	3371	2371	black-brown
v	3315	550	2394	violet, vy. dk.
S	2914	760	2760	salmon
C	1843	3363	2469	pine green, med.
E	4113	422	2673	hazelnut, lt.
◇	4644	316	2316	mauve, med.

	Soie d'Alger	DMC	FT	
Y	3312	554	2396	violet, lt.
⌁	1814	927	2927	gray-green, med.
●	3711	822	2644	beige-gray, lt.
−	2912	950	2950	flesh, lt.
/	3742	613	2613	drab brown, lt.
□	3341	452	2773	shell gray, med.
△	3832	613	2613	drab brown, lt.

22

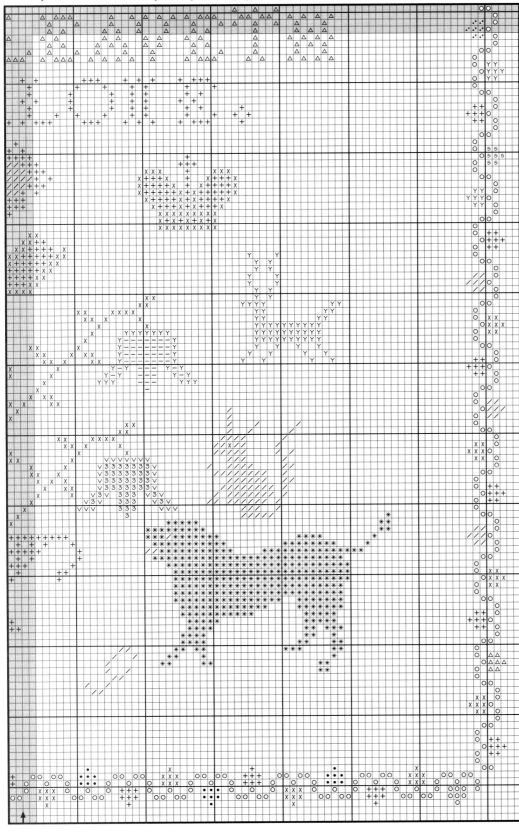

3 3833   372   2579   mustard, lt.

Fabric: 14-count buttermilk cream
stitching paper from Potpourri, Etc.
Stitch count: 243H x 142W
Design size:

14-count	17⅜" x 10⅛"
16-count	15⅛" x 8⅞"
18-count	13½" x 7⅞"
22-count	11" x 6½"

Instructions: Cross stitch using one
strand of silk.

Harriet Hamlet Sampler

This reproduction of the *Harriet Hamlet Sampler* was left unfinished, as was the original. On first glance at the unfinished antique, we pondered if Harriet Hamlet had passed this life before completing her sampler. Upon inspection of the back side of the piece, however, it became apparent that she most likely ran out of materials with which to finish her work. It appears that Harriet began stitching the border about halfway down the right side of her sampler. The satin stitches used at the beginning are packed together densely. As Harriet continued her progress around the perimeter, she must have realized that she would run short of silk with which to complete the design. Beginning down the left side, the stitches are worked much more sparsely than before, and by the time Harriet reached the

Antique—Front

Antique—Back

bottom edge of the border, she was using "economy" satin stitches. Further along this edge, Harriet began substituting a closed Cretan stitch in place of satin, and introduced new floss colors, which appear nowhere else in the design, in the buds of the flowers.

The antique Harriet Hamlet Sampler *features a colorful outer border worked in freehand embroidery. The stitched border remains unfinished, and the markings for completing it can still be seen atop the ground. In addition to her name, age, and the date, Harriet also included the name Pembroke, NH (New Hampshire), which may have been her hometown or, if this was a school piece, the town in which the school was located.*

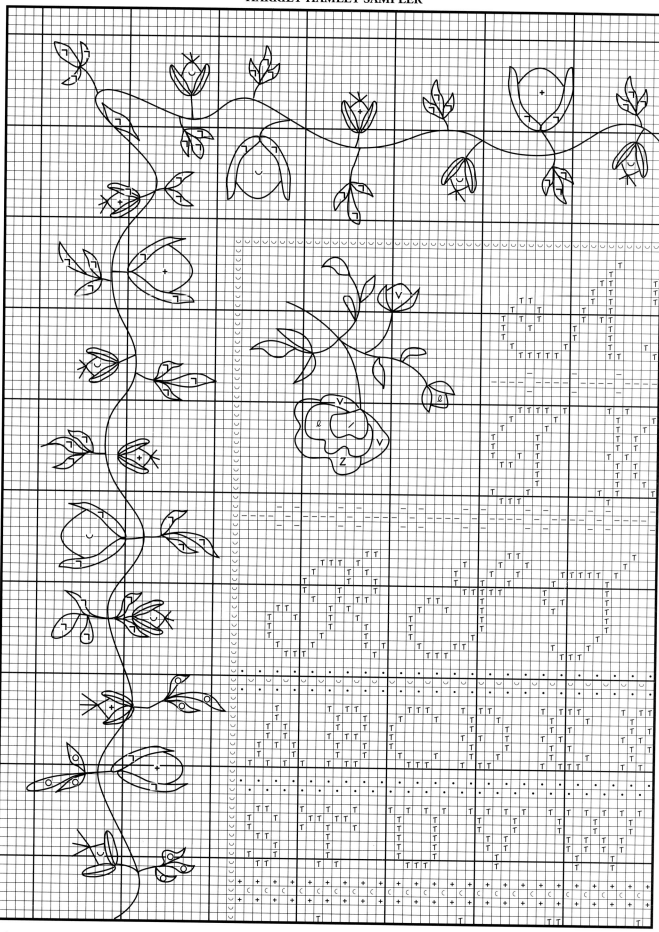

Shaded portion indicates overlap from previous page.

27

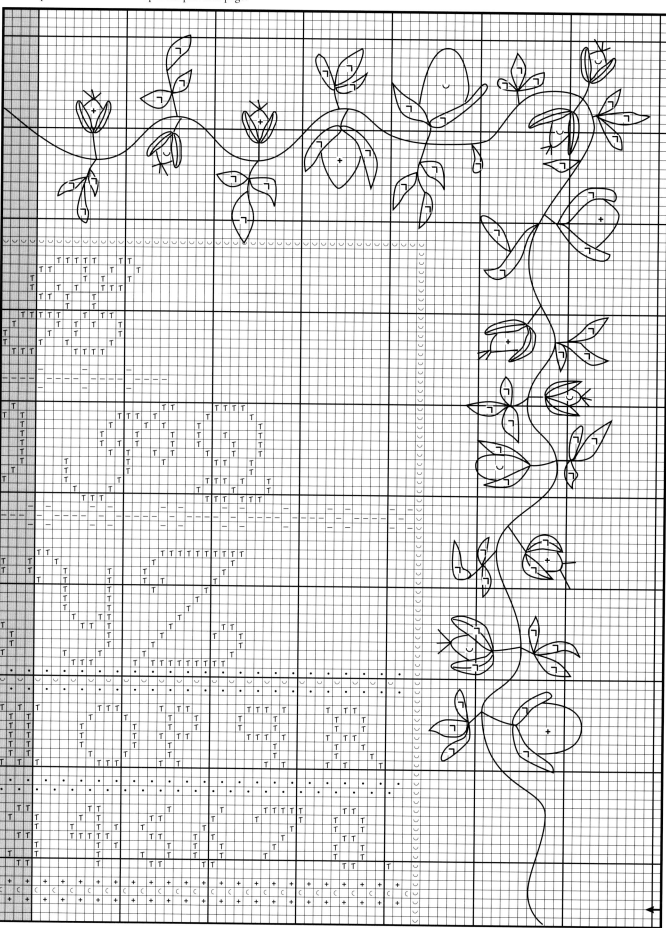

Shaded portion indicates overlap from page 26.

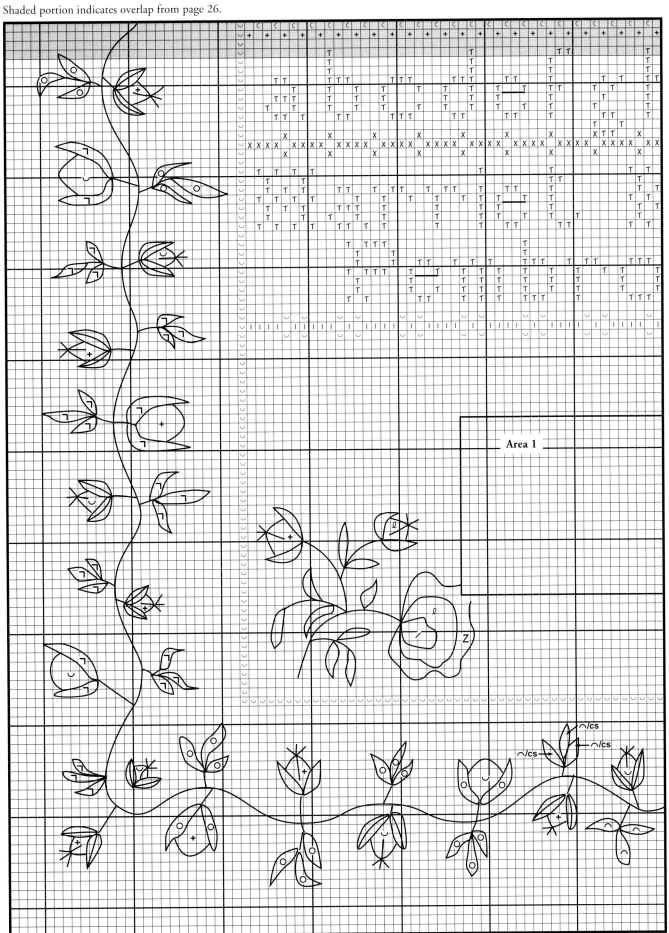

Area 1

Shaded portion indicates overlap from previous page and page 27.

Shaded portion indicates overlap from previous page and page 28.

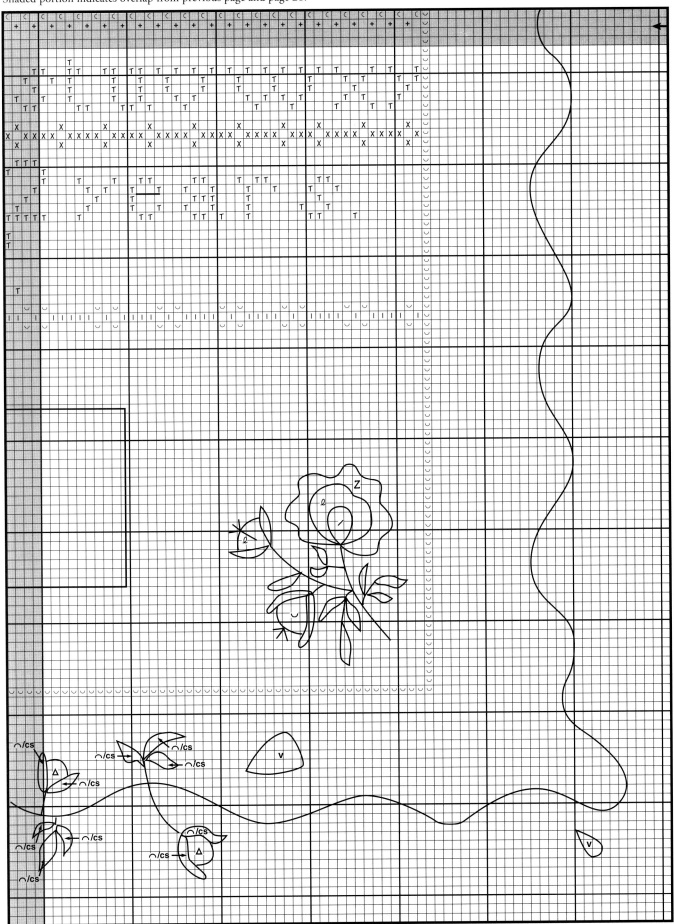

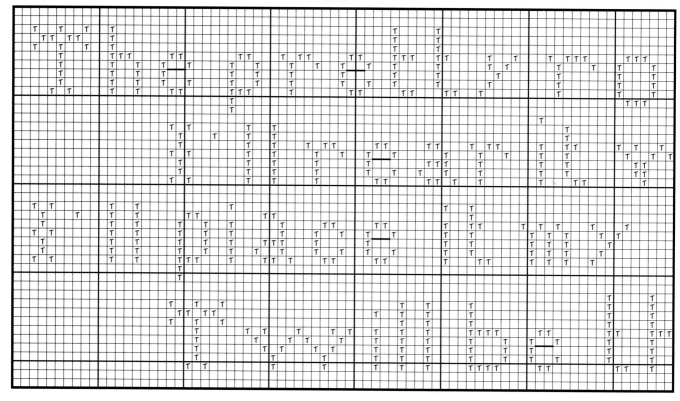

Harriet Hamlet Sampler

Kreinik Soie d'Alger	DMC	DMC FT	
T 4136	3371	2371	black-brown
— 206	924	2924	gray-green, vy. dk.
ı 1442	827	2827	blue, vy. lt.
X 1746	3768	2768	gray-green, dk.
• 526	830	2829	olive, dk.
∪ 3823	437	2738	tan, lt.
+ 3824	436	2436	tan
∩ 204	991	2958	aqua, dk.
v 4622	3688	2572	mauve, med.
△ 2636	3777	2354	terra cotta, vy. dk.
∕ F15	3047	2579	yellow-beige, lt.
ℓ 3825	435	2436	brown, vy. lt.
Z 3742	613	2613	drab brown, lt.
○ 1835	367	2320	pistachio, dk.
⌐ 1844	319	2319	pistachio, vy. dk.
⊂ 1724	931	2931	antique blue, med.

Fabric: 25-count sand Dublin linen from Zweigart®
Stitch count: 192H x 210W
Design size:

25-count	15⅜" x 16⅞"
28-count	13¾" x 15"
32-count	12" x 13⅛"
36-count	10¾" x 11¾"

Instructions: Cross stitch over two threads, using one strand of silk.

Straight-Stitch instructions:
4136 3371 2371 horizontal line on lowercase *e*
206 924 2924 stitches at top of flower buds

Special instructions:
Area 1: Cross stitch over one thread, using one strand of silk.
Flowers inside cross-stitch border:
1. Work open chain stitch for stems, using one strand 206/924/2924.
2. Work satin stitch for leaves, using one strand 206/924/2924.
3. Work satin stitch for flower petals and buds, using one strand of silk.
Outer border:
1. Work chain stitch for vine, using one strand 526/830/2829.
2. Work satin stitch for flower buds, using one strand of silk.
3. Work satin stitch for leaves, using one strand of silk, except along bottom where /CS appears after symbol. Work these leaves in cretan stitch, using one strand of silk. Leaves with dividing stems are worked using one strand 206/924/2924 on outside and one strand 1835/367/2320 on inside.

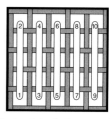

Satin Stitch (Vertical)

Chain Stitch

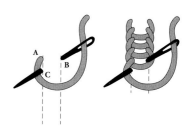

Open Chain Stitch

Shaded portion indicates overlap from previous page.

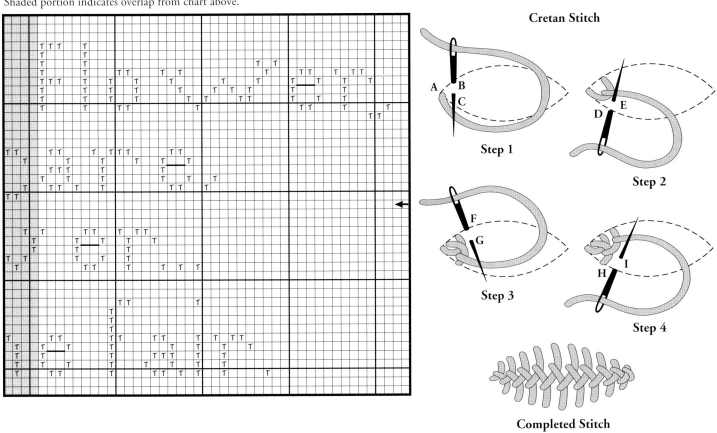

Shaded portion indicates overlap from chart above.

Cretan Stitch

Step 1

Step 2

Step 3

Step 4

Completed Stitch

Sarah Turner Sampler

The Sarah Turner Sampler, *dated 1836, is a charming, uncomplicated piece. The antique has suffered minimal fading through the years, leaving the colors bold and bright. Simple in its design, this sampler includes only a few tree motifs in addition to its variety of alphabets, numerals, and dividing bands.*

Worked with brightly colored flosses that are available to today's stitcher and that closely match the colors of the antique *Sarah Turner Sampler,* this vivid reproduction features row after row of alphabets, numerals, and assorted, decorative dividing bands. Comprised of cross stitch, four-sided stitch, and Algerian eye stitch, this design will be a wonderful project for the beginning sampler stitcher, or for the more advanced needleworker who has just completed a demanding piece and would welcome a less-complicated diversion before beginning her next serious work. As you ply the stitches to create this delightful sampler, note the idiosyncrasies of dropped stitches, as well as changed floss colors in single rows of stitching.

Sarah Turner Sampler

Kreinik

Soie d'Alger	DMC	DMC FT	
X 945	304	2304	red, med.
╱ 1735	414	2414	steel gray, dk.
○ 3441	762	2415	pearl gray, vy. lt.
ı 4644	316	2316	mauve, med.
˥ 3426	501	2501	blue-green, dk.
S 2125	469	2469	avocado
‖ 1846	890	2890	pistachio, ul. dk.
З 1424	311	2337	navy, med.
⌒ 2231	3047	2579	yellow-beige, lt.
4111	738	2738	tan, vy. lt.
916	817	2666	coral red, vy. dk.

DMC Medicis	DMC	DMC FT	
△ 8208	931	2931	antique blue, med.
• 8800	3753	2933	antique blue, ul. vy. lt.

Fabric: 32-count antique tan linen from Wichelt Imports, Inc.
Stitch count: 142H x 116W
Design size:

25-count	11⅜" x 9¼"
28-count	10⅛" x 8¼"
32-count	8⅞" x 7¼"
36-count	7⅞" x 6½"

NOTE: This sampler includes displaced cross stitch. When symbol is placed over a line, the stitch should be placed in that position and worked over two threads.

Instructions: Cross stitch over two threads, using one strand of silk or wool.
Special instructions:
Row 1: Work four-sided stitch using one strand 3441/762/2415 for the letters *I* and the first letter *J,* and one strand 1735/414/2414 for remainder of row.
Row 2: Work four-sided stitch using one strand 945/304/2304 for *O, P, 1, 2,* and *3;* one strand 4111/738/2738 for first *4;* one strand 916/817/2666 for second *4* and remainder of numerals; and one strand 4644/316/2316 for motif at end of row.
Row 3: Work four-sided stitch using one strand 1735/414/2414.
Row 4: Work four-sided stitch using one strand 945/304/2304.
Row 5: Work four-sided stitch using one strand 4644/316/2316 for motif in center of row.
Row 6: Work four-sided stitch using one strand 2231/3047/2579 for the first ten

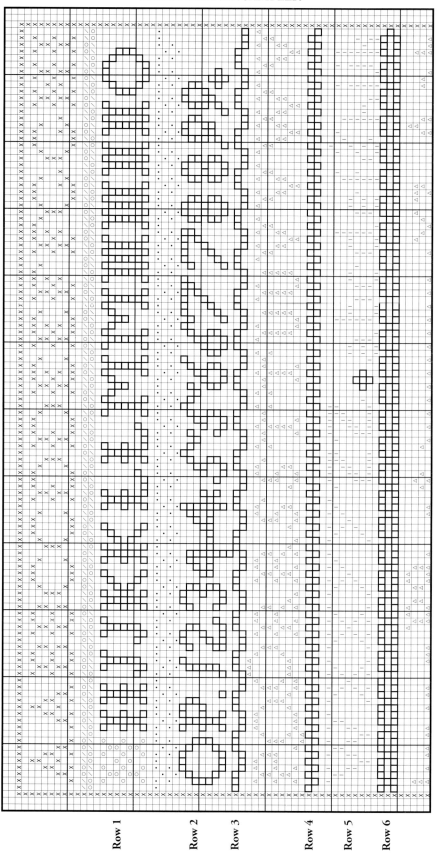

Row 1 Row 2 Row 3 Row 4 Row 5 Row 6

horizontal stitches, and one strand 1735/414/2414 for remainder of row.
Row 7: Work four-sided stitch using one strand 8208/931/2931 for motif between *Z* and *A.*

Row 8: Work four-sided stitches in groups of three, alternating colors across row. Begin with one strand 3426/501/2501 for top half of row and one strand 2231/3047/2579 for bottom half of row.

Shaded portion indicates overlap from previous page.

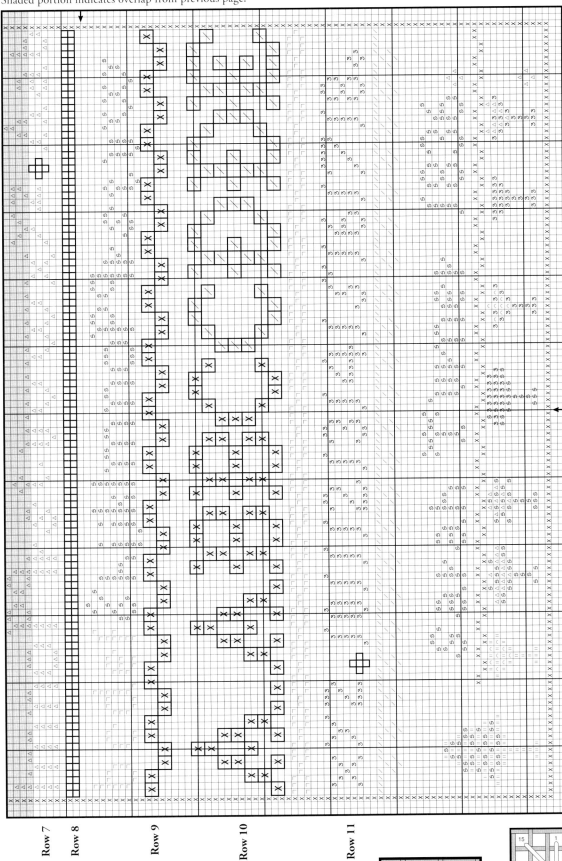

Row 7   Row 8   Row 9   Row 10   Row 11

Rows 9 & 10: Work Algerian eye stitch
using one strand of silk.
Row 11: Work four-sided stitch using one
strand 1424/311/2337 for motif between
Z and *10.*

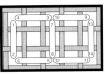

Four-Sided Stitch

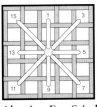

Algerian Eye Stitch

Tudor-Rose Sampler

Brilliant colors create an eye-catching display of stitchery in this stunning *Tudor-Rose Sampler.* Inspired by samplers of the past, this magnificent design will be a treasured addition to the samplermaker's collection. Featuring an abundance of added stitches, this piece will be particularly well-suited to accomplished stitchers. Including cross, diagonal cross, detached buttonhole, rice, satin, eyelet, Montenegrin, double running, Algerian eye, long-armed cross, queen, and four-sided stitches, this vibrant, breathtaking masterpiece will be a prized addition to the enthusiast's collection.

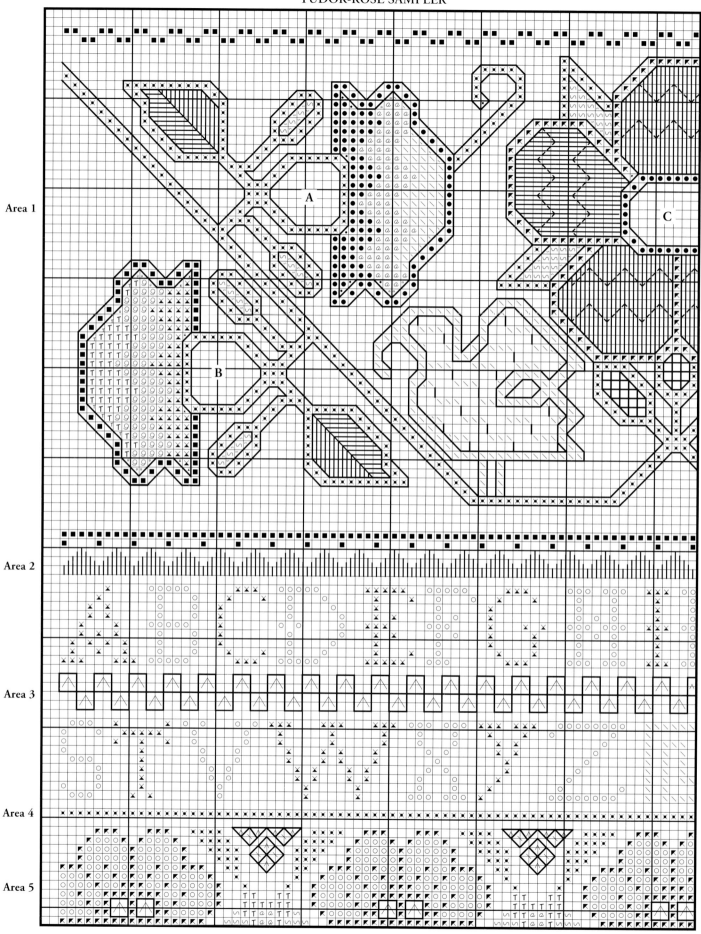

Area 1

A

B

C

Area 2

Area 3

Area 4

Area 5

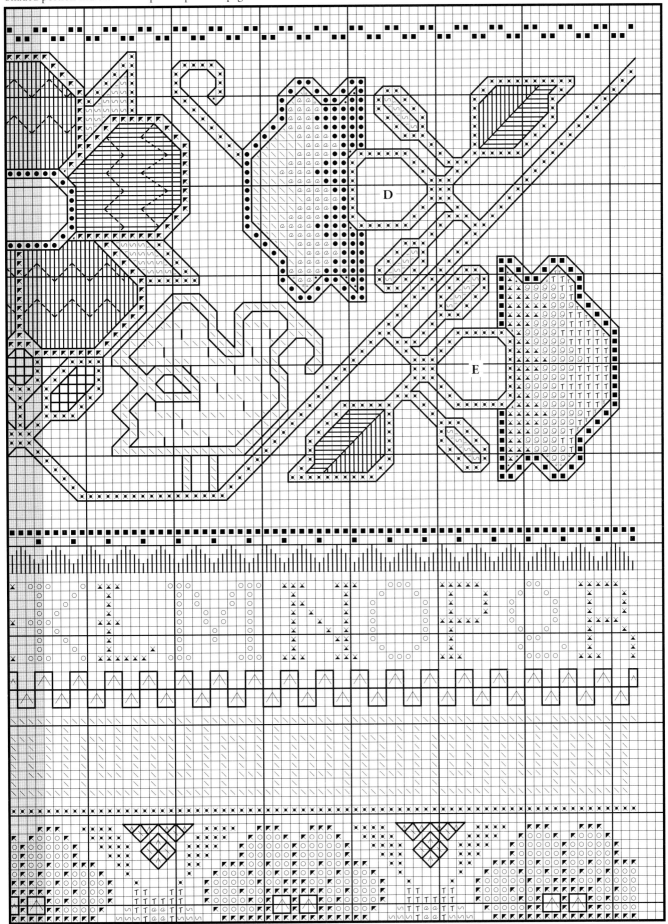

D

E

Shaded portion indicates overlap from page 40.

Area 6

Area 7

Area 8

Area 9

Area 10

Area 11

Area 12

Area 13

Area 14

Area 15

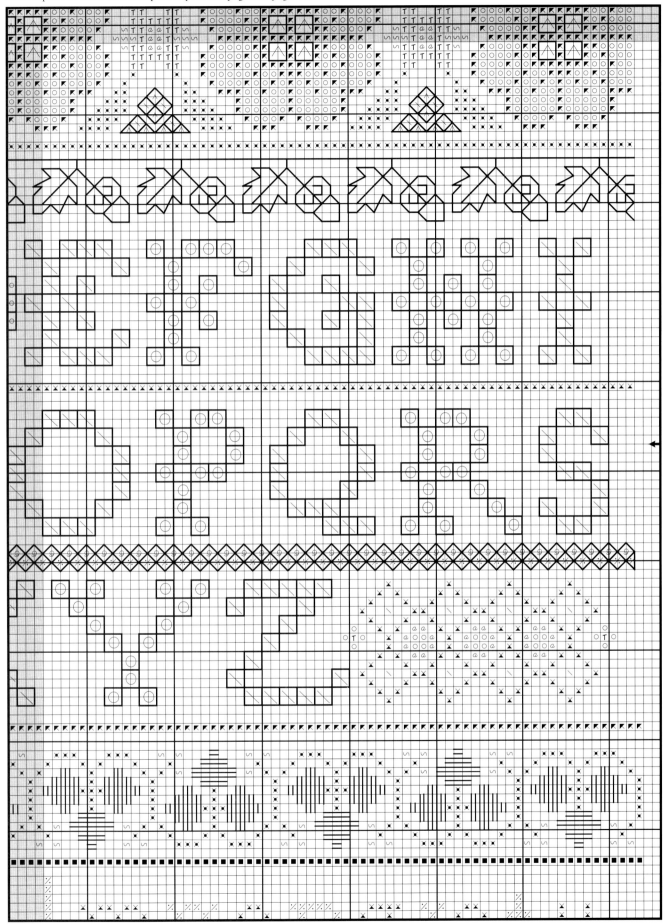

Shaded portion indicates overlap from page 42.

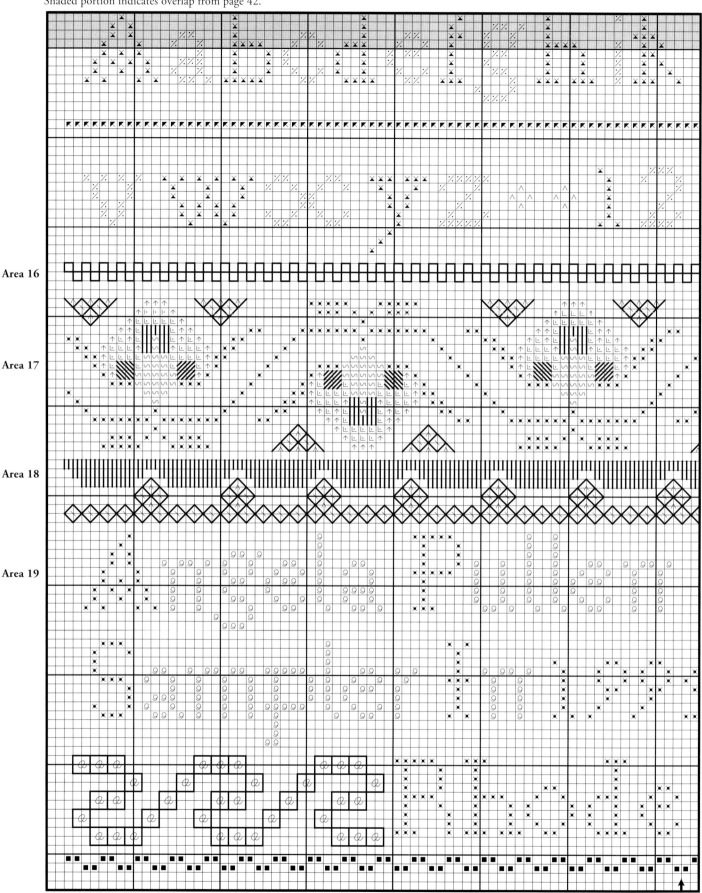

Area 16

Area 17

Area 18

Area 19

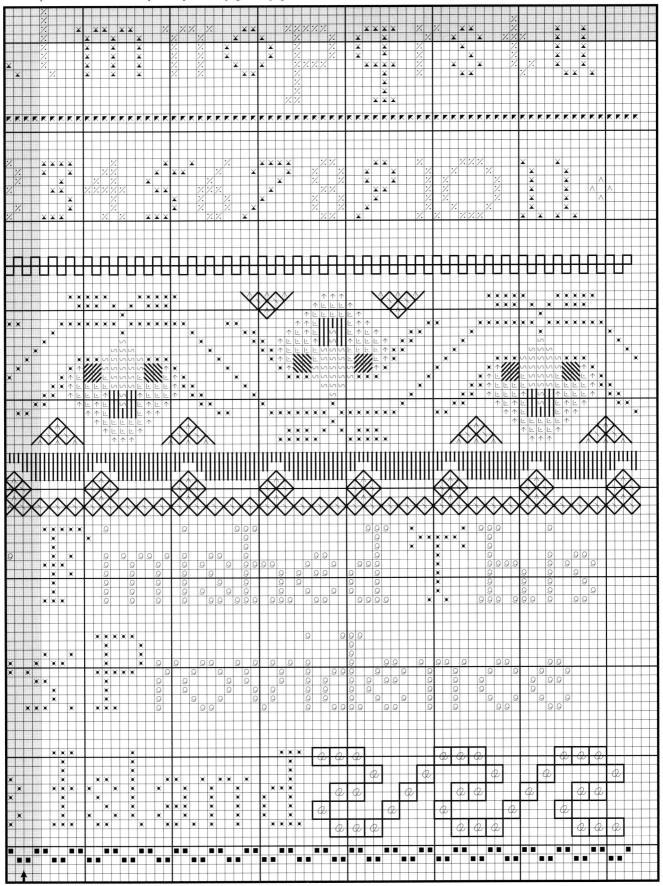

Tudor-Rose Sampler

DMC	Kreinik DMC Soie FT d'Alger		
○ 3328	2329	2915	salmon, med.
✶ 814	2814	2926	garnet, dk.
↑ 3687	2570	3024	mauve
⊾ 3688	3572	4622	mauve, med.
＼ 613	2613	3742	drab brown, lt.
∧ 676	2673	2242	old gold, lt.
ᴄ 729	2783	2533	old gold, med.
• 782	2782	524	topaz, med.
◡ 581	2732	2145	moss green
✖ 890	2890	1846	pistachio, ul. dk.
✗ 930	2930	1715	antique blue, dk.
■ 823	2823	1425	navy, dk.
% 3740	—	—	antique violet, dk.
⊤ 3752	2933	1712	antique blue, vy. lt.
ᴑ 931	2931	1714	antique blue, med.

Fabric: 32-count natural brown undyed linen from Wichelt Imports, Inc.
Stitch count: 290H x 142W
Design size:

25-count	23¼" x 11⅜"
28-count	20¾" x 10⅛"
32-count	18⅛" x 8⅞"
36-count	16⅛" x 7⅞"

Instructions: Cross stitch over two threads, using two strands of floss.
Special instructions:
Area 1: Work diagonal cross stitch for vines, using two strands of floss. Backstitch blue flowers using one strand 823/2823/1425. Work remainder of backstitch using one strand 930/2930/1715. Work detached buttonhole stitch for sections A, B, D, and E, using one strand 890/2890/1846. Work rice stitch for section C, using two strands 782/2782/524 for bottom cross, and two strands 676/2673/2242 for top four corner crosses. Work satin stitch for petals of large flower, stitching in direction indicated by lines on chart. Work inner row using two strands 814/2814/2926, middle row using two strands 3687/2570/3024, and outer row using two strands 3688/3572/4622. Work satin stitch for leaves, using two strands 581/2732/2145 and stitching in direction indicted by lines on chart.
Area 2: Work satin stitch using two strands 729/2783/2533, stitching in direction indicated by lines on chart.
Area 3: Work eyelet stitch using two strands of floss.
Areas 4 & 6: Work Montenegrin stitch using two strands of floss.
Area 5: Work eyelet stitches in center of each flower, using two strands of floss. Work queen stitch using two strands of floss.
Area 7: Work double running stitch for band, using one strand of floss. Work first journey using one strand 676/2673/2242 and second journey using one strand 890/2890/1846. Work double running stitch for leaf, using one strand 676/2673/2242. Work double running stitch for acorn, using one strand 890/2890/1846.
Areas 8, 10, & 12: Work Algerian eye stitch using one strand of floss.
Areas 9, 13, & 15: Work long-armed cross stitch using two strands of floss.
Area 11: Work queen stitch using two strands of floss.
Area 14: Work satin stitch for flowers, using two strands of floss and stitching in direction indicated by lines on chart. For first flower, stitch lower petals using 3687/2570/3024 and upper petal using 3688/3572/4622. For second flower, stitch upper petals using 814/2814/2926 and lower petal using 3687/2570/3024. Alternate flower colors across band.
Area 16: Work four-sided stitch using one strand 823/2823/1425.
Area 17: Work queen stitch using two strands of floss. Work satin stitch in center of each flower, using two strands 814/2814/2926 and stitching in direction indicated by lines on chart.
Area 18: Work satin stitch for band, using two strands 613/2613/3742 and stitching in direction indicated by lines on chart. Work queen stitch using two strands of floss.
Area 19: Personalize using sampler alphabets and numerals, using two strands 890/2890/1846 for uppercase letters and two strands 931/2931/1714 for lowercase letters. Work eyelet stitch using two strands of floss.

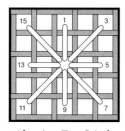

Algerian Eye Stitch

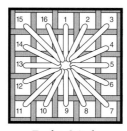

Eyelet Stitch

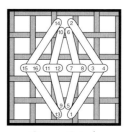

Queen Stitch

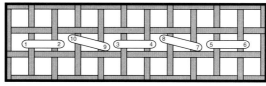

Double Running Stitch

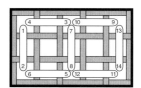

Four-Sided Stitch

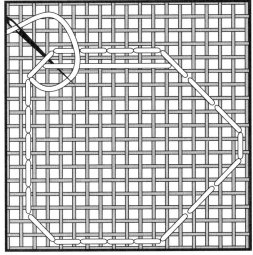

Detached Buttonhole Stitch—Step 1

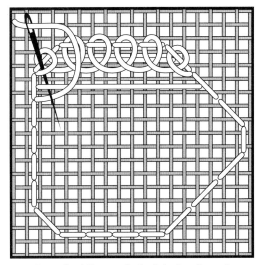

Detached Buttonhole Stitch—Step 2

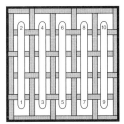

Satin Stitch (Vertical)

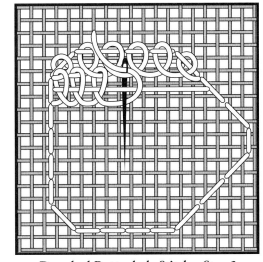

Detached Buttonhole Stitch—Step 3

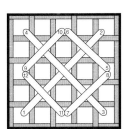

Rice Stitch

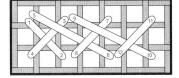

Long-Armed Cross Stitch

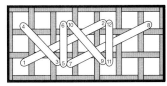

Montenegrin Stitch

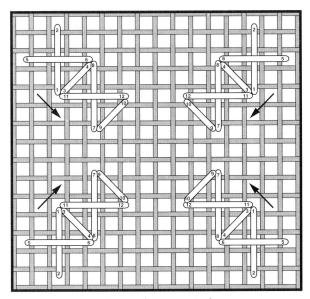

Diagonal Cross Stitch

Diagonal Cross Stitch—Turning Corners

Joshua and Caleb Sampler

This interesting stitchery features a popular sampler motif, based on the Biblical story of Joshua and Caleb, as its central focus. Designed to fit within the frame of an elegant candle screen, this small sampler includes several over-one cross-stitch sections and an assortment of specialty stitches. Candle screens were designed to shield women's faces from the heat of candle flames, which were used as a light source before the invention of electricity. Because the makeup women wore during those days was wax-based, protection from the heat of the flame was essential to prevent milady's cosmetics from melting.

Inspired by samplers from days gone by, this attractive design features Joshua and Caleb, a motif that was frequently used on antique samplers. A variety of stitches and over-one sections add interest and charm to this delightful piece.

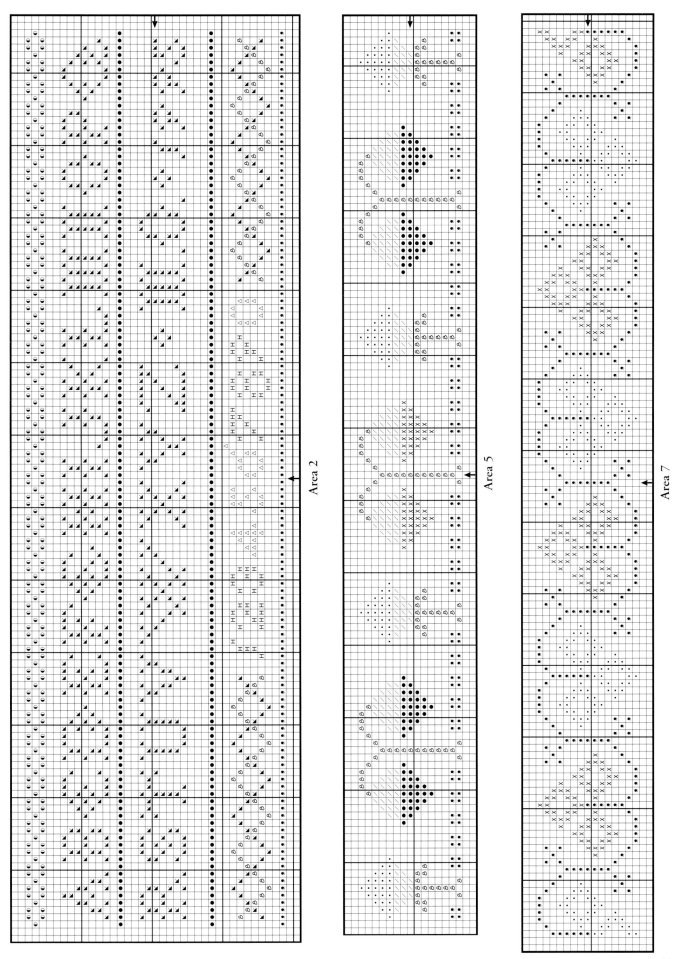

Area 2

Area 5

Area 7

49

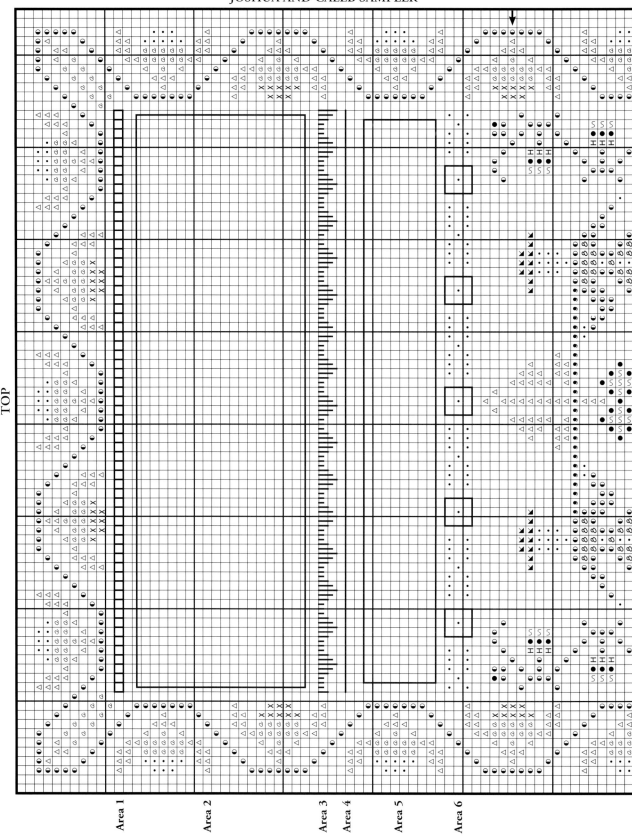

TOP

Area 1 Area 2 Area 3 Area 4 Area 5 Area 6

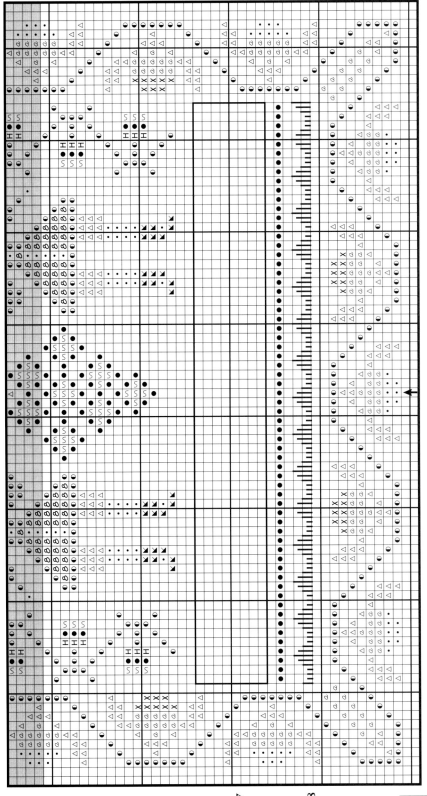

Area 7

Area 8

Joshua and Caleb Sampler

	DMC	Kreinik FT	DMC Soie d'Alger	
8	3364	2471	1831	pine green
∕	524	—	3423	fern green, vy. lt.
ƙ	930	2930	1736	antique blue, dk.
◑	3362	2937	3726	pine green, dk.
H	3802	—	—	mauve, vy. dk.
●	934	—	3726	avocado-black
X	3328	2329	2915	salmon, med.
ᐧ	ecru	ecru	brut	ecru
ꕷ	3042	—	3323	antique violet, lt.
ᶜ	758	2758	922	terra cotta, lt.
△	3363	2469	3723	pine green, med.
●	3041	—	—	antique violet, med.

Fabric: 32-count antique tan linen from Wichelt Imports, Inc.

Stitch count: 107H x 81W

Design size:

28-count	7⅝" x 5¾"
30-count	7⅛" x 5⅜"
32-count	6⅝" x 5"
36-count	6" x 4½"

Instructions: Cross stitch over two threads, using two strands of floss unless other-wise indicated.

Special instructions:

Area 1: Work four-sided stitch using one strand 3041/—/—.

Areas 2, 5, & 7: Cross stitch over one thread, using one strand of floss.

Area 3: Work satin stitch using two strands 3802/—/—.

Area 4: Backstitch using one strand 930/2930/1736.

Area 6: Work eyelet stitch in boxed areas, using one strand of floss.

Area 8: Work satin stitch using two strands 524/—/3423.

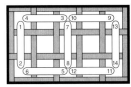

Four-Sided Stitch

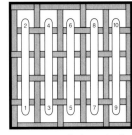

Eyelet Stitch   **Satin Stitch (Vertical)**

Chatelaines:
Traveling Companions of an Intimate Persuasion

In medieval France, the mistress of the house (castle, chateau) wore as her badge of position, the keys to the estate, the larder, the wine cellar—whatever keys were necessary to the safekeeping of her husband's or, in some cases, her employer's, property. Her title was *la châtelaine* and, in order to keep her keys readily available, as well as secure, she appended them at the waist of her garment. Through time, the title of the person was given over to the implements of her authority. Although the needlewoman knows the chatelaine as a wearable ornament that holds a needlecase and thimble bucket, a tape measure, scissors sheath, and a pincushion, the tool collection is only one of a number of such items. Not only are there single-purpose chatelaines for the seamstress, holding only one tool, but also there are those appropriately adapted for both men and women of other interests.

The term *chatelaine* appeared in print in the April 1828 issue of *The World of Fashion,* a magazine published in London during most of the nineteenth century. Cummins and Taunton, in their comprehensive work on chatelaines and like accessories, offer this quote as the earliest employ of both word and specialized definition:

> Several ladies wear, attached to their girdles, a gold clasp, surmounted by a coronet, either that of a duke, a count or a marquis. Beneath the crown is a ring from which is suspended a chain terminated by a cap; this cap supports three or four other chains; to every one of which is attached a gold key. The largest chain of gold is called *la Châtelaine.*

Within nine months of this fashion news, the same periodical described the fashion accessory as the bearer of a scent bottle and other handsome trinkets.

Before the word *chatelaine* actually appeared in print as a part of stylish dress, similar appendages were employed for the same purposes, and it is a question of semantics as to their appropriate appellation. Certainly swords and daggers were held in sheaths at the sides of warriors; purses or bags to hold script and documents were suspended from cord and leather belts; the Chinese of the sixteenth century B.C. wore writing implements at the waist. Pomanders filled with aromatic mixtures, both pleasing and suffocating, were prescribed by physicians and pharmacists, especially during the years of the "Black Death" (the bubonic plague), to ward off disease, and these found their way around a person's neck, waist, and even wrists and ankles. Clearly the modern collector would defer from identifying a sword scabbard as a chatelaine appendage, but sixteenth-century "escarcelles" (pouches) and pendant needle and thimble cases qualify under today's definition. Nevertheless,

*Silver-plated Art Nouveau disc pincushion **(above left)** from a late-nineteenth-century chatelaine. The original cushion of royal-purple velveteen is still intact. **(Above right)** Gold vermeil watch chatelaine marked "60, ie, omy-." The design is mid nineteenth century but the origin is uncertain.*

the purist will want to be watchful for the word *equipage* in her research, for it was the eighteenth-century term for a chain-bearing fashion complement that was hung at the waist. The equipage usually sported an "étui," a portable case for assorted grooming, sewing, and/or writing necessities. However, the word *étui* sometimes defined both the case and the cord or chain to which it was attached, and then there were étuis constructed without the thought of connection to anything at all. Purses linked to a belt or hanging from the waist, sometimes stretching almost to the ground, were called "aumonieres," and it may be that discovery of a reference to such an item will lead to information about the chatelaine. "Portmonnaie" carries the same significance. The diligent student of needlework tools will undoubtedly find references and cross references for chatelaines and their appendages, as well as the identification of similar and dissimilar items, by a number of names. Purveyors of antique needlework tools seem to class all such items, a plaque or "head" with a waist clasp from which assorted tools and accessories are hung by chains, as chatelaines.

In addition to needlework chatelaines, there were those specifically designed for holding watches, scent bottles, fans, "porte-jupes" (skirt lifters), spectacles, parasols, and keys. Nurses and nannies had chatelaines that held the assorted instruments of their professions. The sporting set carried accessories for tennis and archery; tiny pens, pencils, and even a palette of watercolors were available to the mobile artist. Muffs and dainty handkerchiefs hung from chains and cords fitted with hooks or clever clamps. At the height of this fashion trend, the clever merchant found a way to accommodate every possible client.

It should be noted that the major manufacturers of chatelaines were jewelers. Some created all of the implements and baubles that completed the piece, while others used scissors from a cutler or mirrors from a glazier. Although one thinks of precious metals and costly stones as jewelers' materials, in the case of chatelaines and other toys,[1] faceted steel, vermeil, and brass were not beyond the jewelers' artistic sensibilities. The baser metals afforded the middle and merchant classes, of the

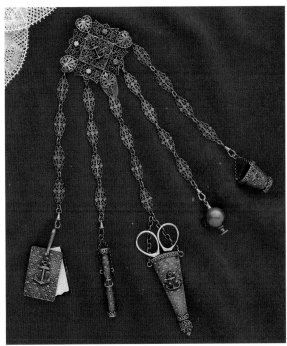

nineteenth century in particular, the opportunity to follow fashion trends and, at one point, faceted steel was the rage among even the crustiest of the upper crust.

Attention to ornament in dress and jewelry became more intense during the sixteenth century. The English took a particular interest in the styles of the continent and, as political marriages were arranged, court amenities from various nations were introduced and intermingled. The manner of dress, personal adornment, and home decor reached a point that might be called gaudy by today's standards; historians call it baroque. One need look no further than the portraits of Henry VIII, or Elizabeth I, as well as those of her nobles and courtiers, to see some of the most elaborate needlework and lavish jewelry ever produced. The description of a bedroom's decor at Hardwick Hall, the favorite residence of Bess of Hardwick, combines two shades of brilliant red curtains for the bed with a bright green chair of quilted satin. (This same Bess is the one who delighted her monarch with intricately embroidered sleeves and skirt covers rather than the traditional gold cups proffered as New Year's gifts.) England's Elizabethan Age was one of excess, and the same taste was to be found among those in France and Spain, Italy, and what are now modern Germany and Austria. Style, by virtue of its high-born progenitors, was mimicked by every class, from tavern maid to aristocrat. While the wealthy wore gold watches, nutmeg graters, and étuis dangling from engraved and bejeweled chains, the poor wore knitted pin balls and reticules suspended

Late-nineteenth-century chatelaine of oxidized and gilt metals. The symbols for the Biblical "Faith, Hope, and Charity" are incorporated in its design by the use of the anchor, cross, and heart. The tape measure may not be an original appendage. The aide-mémoire contains notes about a ship voyage on which the owner was seasick!

from waist cords and leather belts. The seventeenth century did not see a curtailment of the taste for elaborate attire. Extant paintings and advertisements of the period depict both ladies and gentlemen in lace-trimmed collars, flamboyant hats, and lengthy chatelaines holding watches, knives, keys, and purses. The ladies' chatelaines held fans and muffs, mirrors and pomanders.

Indeed, the eighteenth century found the chatelaine's popularity at its zenith. Toymakers, jewelers, and watchmakers advertised a plethora of designs and assorted matching

*S*ilver chatelaine with scissors in sheath, disc pincushion, button hook, thimble bucket, and small purse. English, c. 1890; **2)** Silver needlecase with friction closure. English, late nineteenth century; **3)** Silver fausse montre. English, late eighteenth century; **4)** Collapsible scissors in a sheath. The scissors are so securely held by the sheath that the attachment ring is at its bottom and the scissors hang upside down. They are larger than needlework scissors and may have dangled from a specialty, single-purpose chatelaine; **5)** Aide-mémoire with lavender enamel covers. The leaves are of ivory and a tiny, mechanical pencil is attached to the side of one of the covers. Probably American, early twentieth century.
Photography by Edmonson and Father

appendages in baroque and then rococo designs that can be labeled nothing short of glorious. Quotidian models of pierced and faceted steel were elaborate in their construction, but those of gold went beyond elaborate to something like luxurious. They were set with diamonds, enameled in brilliant colors, and even embraced diminutive, Wedgwood plaques. Tiny, decorative tassels were constructed of minuscule gold links to hang on either side of a watch with a repoussé cover, or lilliputian portraits, as well as "homely" scenes, which were fashioned into the links and watch cases. Watch keys and cranks, seals, and other useful appendages still swung from the chatelaine's chains, but newer items, which were no more than ornamental, appeared near the close of the century. Rather like the charm bracelets so popular during the middle of the present century, chatelaines took on breloques (trinkets or charms including tassels) that imitated horns, butterflies, harps, and even miniature household items such as teapots, kettles, and baskets. A particularly interesting accessory that appeared during this period was the "fausse montre," which often duplicated a chatelaine's watch but had no works inside. It could be used by the bearer to carry whatever suited his or her needs.

In the last quarter of the eighteenth century, the macaroni appeared. This hookless chain, which was looped over the belt or waistband, usually held a watch at one end and often a fausse montre at the other. Usually made of gold and embellished with enamel, precious stones, and delicate plaques, the macaroni acquired its name from the new and very popular pasta being enjoyed in London. Anything new and smart, including a dandy who wore a "feather in his hat," was called "macaroni," so of course this alternative chatelaine acquired the name and, of the many fads and fashions with which it shared the approbation, only it retained the moniker. The links of the chain or composite of chains from which the macaroni was assembled were fashioned so that both sides were equally adorned. The attached watch was allowed to hang free, which was not always the case with other chatelaines that served more as a fob for a timepiece secured in a pocket. It is difficult to imagine the delicate beauty of Wedgwood mixed with steel chains, but existing in the Powerhouse Museum, Sydney, Australia, are two macaroni chatelaines of such a combination. One features a tile design with a faceted-steel bead in the center; the other shows two figures in profile, one of which is seated.[2]

The first decades of the nineteenth century, when empire gowns were in vogue, have been considered to be a period when women's use of chatelaines declined. Fashion plates and advertisements of the time, however, seem to contradict the notion. It is difficult to imagine giving up a purse or bag, and certainly not a timepiece, for the sake of fashion. Chains draped between two hooks attached at the raised waistline, or simply looped over the belt or dress sash at either end, still served women as pendant-holding accessories. As the century progressed, plaques without chains, or with a single ring attached, served as guardians of watches and breloques. With the return of full skirts and normal waistlines, longer chatelaines enjoyed a resurgence in popularity. Those sported by French gentlemen did not hang from the waist, as did those of their female counterparts, but rather from a pocket in their waistcoats. From the chains dangled such an assortment of ornaments that an article in an 1849 English publication decried the non-utilitarian appendages as the ultimate absurdity, and closed with an ardent wish that the fashion would not cross the channel. It did.

Victorian ladies continued to wear chatelaines, both new and old, the latter apparently retrieved from their mother's and grandmother's jewelry boxes. They were displayed in great numbers at the 1851 Great Exhibition, and by 1870, they were so enthusiastically embraced, even by royalty, that those articles once carried in vestment pockets were hung from assorted chains. A variation of the chatelaine, popularized by the Prince and Princess of Wales, was the Norwegian belt. The belt was constructed of several pieces of leather, joined together by metal links from which chains were suspended for the convenient transport of toiletries and watches, purses and vinaigrettes, aide-mémoires, and other useful and "necessary" items. The belt was made so

Silver chatelaine with plaque of helmeted male figure flanked by griffins. The appendages include a disc pincushion, scissor sheath, retractable wooden pencil, and thimble bucket. English, late nineteenth century.
Photography by Edmonson and Father

Gilt- and oxidized-metal chatelaine with six chains, which hold a reel pincushion, a needlecase, an aide-mémoire, a scissor sheath, a retractable pencil, and a tiny silver locket with a Madonna figure on the lid. The pincushion and aide-mémoire are well-matched and the scissor sheath is of like manufacture, but the lovely components are not all original to the plaque that holds them. Obviously they reflect the taste of the owner, or have been added to complete the piece by a merchant or collector. Each piece is English, with the exception of the locket, which may be Spanish.
Photography by Edmonson and Father

that two sets of chains fell close to the sides of the wearer. The double set of chains lent itself to matched pairs of accoutrements, especially purses and writing implements. The variety of chatelaines available at the end of the century was without limit. They not only imitated those of their ancestors, but incorporated the artistry of foreign countries and colonies. The British Empire encompassed so much of the world that it is sufficient to say the taste of every subject could be satisfied with one chatelaine design or another. Sylvia Groves, one of the earliest students of needlework tools, notes that even chatelaines of jet were constructed for those who were in mourning. Considering Victoria's life-long grief over the loss of her beloved Albert, and the realm's sympathetic relationship to Her Majesty, the use of black is not surprising. During Victoria's reign, even straight pins for affixing collars and cuffs to clothing were produced in black.

A trend that began during the nineteenth century and that continues today is the decoration of chatelaine appendages by the women

Silver chatelaine with waist plaque designed to resemble a Japanese fan. Hallmarks indicate that it was made in London by "C. B." in 1888. The appendages were fashioned by the same jeweler, but in 1887. One may only speculate about the mixture.

who wear them. Embroidered reticules first appeared around 1840; needlebooks, scissor sheaths, and thimble holders are still being embroidered by modern needlewomen who then attach them to another variation of the chatelaine, a weighted fabric tape that is draped about the shoulder. A contest in Australia in 1992, the Margaret Oppen Competition, produced modern pieces that more accurately resemble the earlier chatelaines, using ribbon, and twisted and crocheted cords, in the place of chains. The history buff and needlework-tool aficionado will be pleased to find in current publications new variations on the old theme of portable instruments appropriate to his or her particular persuasion.

The descendants of the chatelaine, which no longer bear the name, are still employed by both men and women. Consider the volume of keys attached to a belt or belt loop by a spiraling cord that ends in a ring, or the recent revival of scent bottles worn about the neck.

A version of the chatelaine that continued well into this century was that of the specialty chatelaine. There were watch chatelaines that became shorter as time passed and eventually were worn on the bodice of the dress. For men, they still looped across the vest of a three-piece suit, terminating in a watch pocket, and midway on the chain often dangled a charm or special memento. Near the turn of the century, professional societies often awarded men of merit engraved gold pieces, shaped much like tiny plaques, to attach to watch fobs. Other single-purpose chatelaines with lone appendages were those used to hold perfume or scent bottles. They were produced in a variety of clever shapes to hold, in addition to appealing fragrances, smelling salts, and were, during the late nineteenth century, occasionally referred to as "smelling bottles." Besides the flask shape, which was no less beautifully constructed despite its predictable configuration, there were cassolettes or "flacons à sel" fashioned to appear as tiny pistols, quivers of arrows, and sheathed daggers.

As far back as the sixteenth century, ladies suspended fans from their waists; in 1900, fans still hung from silk ribbons attached to waist plaques. The fans were made of everything from ostrich feathers to silk; their ribs made of ivory, bone, and several manners of wood. Those made of sandalwood were particularly popular because of their fragrance.

Perhaps one of the most delightful single-purpose chatelaines was that which held an aide-mémoire. While the tiny tablet was often found on chatelaines bearing multiple appendages, there were also those that accompanied ladies as sole companions. They first had pages of wafer-thin ivory, which gave over to celluloid; then plastic and, finally, vellum. To find one in which the notes of an early owner still survive affords the collector an opportunity to know more intimately the lady who wore it. Some still contain snatches of poetry, the sentiments of the gift giver, or notes about a pattern or recipe. Made of as many materials as other chatelaines, the little tablets were sometimes shaped to appear as a book, with a pencil hidden in the hinge or held by a sheath that was made of small cylinders, alternately attached to the covers, so that the inserted pencil held the book closed.

The "porte jupe" was a fashionable way to lift one's long skirt from the dust or mud of a busy street, or to facilitate dancing at a social gathering. Basically, this skirt-lifter was a clamp of any of several designs, suspended from the waist by a chain or ribbon. Clever manufacturers gave them titles like "The Grappler" or "The Surprise," and offered them with adjustable chains of simple or elaborate design. Nothing could be more feminine than to hold up one's gown with a length of silver butterflies or flowers! Today wedding dresses and debutante gowns incorporate a loop of fabric, which slips over the wrist of the wearer, in the seam of the skirt or the train. As she raises her arm to dance, the folds of fabric are rescued from errant footsteps. Perhaps more practical, this adaptation of the porte jupe is far less lovely.

Chatelaines have carried parasols and spectacles, purses and medical tools. Spectacle chatelaines were worn at the waist or on the dress bodice. The majority held a lozenge-shaped receptacle, which was open at the top for easy retrieval of the glasses. Nurses' chatelaines, worn at the waist, usually carried several types of scissors, a spatula, forceps, and sometimes a pencil. Early styles simply let the tools or

A product of the first decade of the twentieth century, when dressmakers made house calls, this silver chatelaine (**top left**) holds an aide-mémoire, a fountain-pen case, and a bucket pincushion. Not what one might consider a sewing chatelaine, the appendage configuration lends itself to the realm of the seamstress; although the unmatched parts indicate that the assemblage came from several sources, and was not designed as a unit for a specific activity. If, indeed, this was not the possession of a needleworker, the three tools simply met the particular needs of its owner. The pen case is constructed with a sliding-chain arrangement that holds both parts of the container, similar to the configuration of oriental needle-cases, and was advertised as a "registered device" in 1907. (**Left**) Silver spool knave with spring pin for attachment to garment. Made in Birmingham, England in 1911, it is a descendent of those knaves used for tambouring.

implements hang free, but later, leather pouches were fitted with the tools in the manner of a sewing case.

Unusual and rather cumbersome were ring chatelaines for wrist or finger. Although a few were made early in the nineteenth century, the majority of those manufactured appeared at the end of that century and at the beginning of the next. They were advertised as both novel and useful because they could be worn on the finger or wrist, or might be attached to a plaque at the waist. It is difficult to imagine a compendium of tools hanging from one's finger, and apparently the practice was not only uncomfortable but impractical. The fad did not enjoy a long life.

Sewing chatelaines are, to the needlewoman, the only true chatelaines. Of course, this is due

to the fact that they are still constructed by and for needlewomen, and therefore are more familiar to them. They hold a greater variety of tools than most chatelaines; tools that are common to every needleworker, as well as those that serve the particular needs for a special interest. Most of these wonderful items make scissors, needles, and a thimble readily available. Others add knives, reels, bodkins, emeries, ball or disc or bucket-style pincushions. Some have winding tape measures, stilettos, and aide-mémoires. There are those that hold only knitting-needle guards

 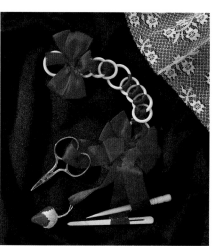

Ring and ribbon-work chatelaine of brass rings and pale green silk (above left). The only appendages are a velveteen pincushion and a silk emery. It is unusual that brass rings were employed rather than plastic or celluloid. Circa 1902. The Merry Cox Collection. (Above right) Ribbon-and-ring chatelaine of brilliant red silk and plastic or celluloid rings. The stiletto and emery are older than the bodkin. The scissors are of recent manufacture. The original parts are probably early twentieth century. The Merry Cox Collection.

and those that, when hung from the wrist, hold balls of thread or yarn for crocheting, knitting, or tambouring. The earlier models were usually the porters of étuis, in which vertical slots held a range of tools, the scissors having folding or collapsible bows (handles) to make them smaller and more easily stored. Purveyors of nineteenth-century needlework chatelaines followed the same practice that they did with chatelaines of fashion. Heads or plaques were often sold individually so that the needlewoman could select those tools

particularly helpful to her. They were matched in design, as were those non-needlework appendages, and it is not uncommon to find a chatelaine with needlework tools with perhaps a scent bottle or a button hook or even a folding corkscrew hanging among them.

Most sewing chatelaines bear their longest chain in the middle of several shorter chains, and from it hangs a scissor sheath or a scissor case with a hinged top. There may be as many as nine individual chains, although this is rare, or two or three major chains that then hold secondary chains. Odd numbers of appendages are the norm; even numbers rare. The folding travel scissors that are still in use today were found on chatelaines as early as 1892, but were unusual for that time. Finding an antique sewing chatelaine with the original scissors in their holder is difficult; collectors should carefully match markings and be familiar with period design to assure authenticity when purchasing a piece that includes scissors and/or thimble. The absence of either or both items does not make a chatelaine uncollectible; rather their presence adds to its value.

Thimbles, like scissors, may be held in a container called a thimble bucket, and it looks just like that for which it is named: a bucket. Others are contained in a cylindrical, hinged case, with a top that has a snap or friction closure. (In rare cases, these containers had screw tops, but few are found today outside museum collections.) Inside the case, one usually finds a tiny spindle with a mushroom-shaped cap on it, upon which the thimble sits. Thread containers, sometimes called cotton barrels, often look just like the thimble case from the outside, but they may be differentiated by the lack of the inner spindle and a tiny groove near the closure, from which the thread may be pulled. Popular shapes for both items, in addition to the cylinder, are acorns and eggs. Needle and bodkin cases may have any of the closing mechanisms that are found on the thimble and thread containers, but the majority have friction closures. Bodkins are generally longer than needles, and a chatelaine with only one such case is probably meant to hold needles. A pair of containers usually indicates that one is for needles; the other for a bodkin. Twentieth-century chatelaines are more likely to have needlebooks than needlecases, holding within their covers several leaves to hold different sizes or styles of needles. Some hang open; some are held closed by a tiny length of ribbon or cording. Antique needlecases from chatelaines will have a ring, usually at the top of the case, from which it was appended. Those without a ring are probably from workboxes or étuis.

There are generally three types of pincushions found on chatelaines: disc, reel, and bucket. The disc cushion is constructed of two geometrically identical pieces of material, usually metal, between which is sandwiched a fabric-covered cushion. The reel pincushion is fashioned in the same manner, but through its center is a tiny axle allowing the cushion to be turned like a little wheel. The bucket pincushion is not as common as others and it may be shaped in a configuration other than that of a bucket; perhaps a small crescent or the popular acorn would be used to hold the actual cushion. More contemporary chatelaines have ball-style cushions that have no fittings of other materials by which to attach them to chains or ribbons.

Tape measures on antique chatelaines are often spherical or cylindrical, with a protruding knob that turns a spool within the casing. This allows the rewinding of the tape after use. If the piece holds an étui, there may be a folding tape measure inside it. The author has found a spring-retractable tape measure on a nurse's chatelaine, but not on a sewing chatelaine. The tape inside a container may be of silk or cotton ribbon with marks for linear measure printed or drawn on it.

Collectors who carefully inspect chatelaines may find a few charming surprises. Occasionally one appendage may serve as two tools. A needlecase may have a thimble as its top, or a stiletto's handle may serve as a bodkin case. A twentieth-century piece that holds a darning egg or glove darner may also serve as a recept-

acle for needles or a tiny spindle upon which thread is wound.

Most chatelaines are of European manufacture, although some are of American origin. American products are more likely than their foreign counterparts to have a pin, rather than a clasp, with which to affix them to clothing and to hold among their appendages an emery. Chinese chatelaines have appendages with covers that slide up and down the chains or cords to protect the tools when they are not in use. They are often decorated with silk tassels, lovely beads, and delicate embroidery. Tibetan pendant needlecases are extant, but Japanese sewing chatelaines are unknown. (The Japanese did carry items, usually pouches, suspended from their waists, but needlework tools were seldom

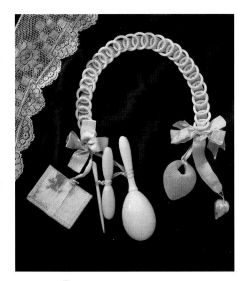 

*Chatelaine constructed of ribbon and plastic rings (**above left**). The heart-shaped pincushion is of velveteen; the strawberry emery and the needlebook are covered with a silk print. The sock and glove darners are made of wood, but the stiletto, which is fashioned like a manicuring tool, may have come from a grooming kit. Instructions for making chatelaines of this style were featured in late-nineteenth- and early-twentieth-century ladies' magazines. The maker of this particular piece probably used those pieces and fabric scraps already in her possession. (**Above right**) Creamy silk fabric and ribbon compose this offspring of the chatelaine. It has a ribbon embroidery wreath, which incorporates a tiny calla lily, in the center of the base portion. The extra ribbon at either end of the base suggests that it might be tied to a belt at the waist. Appendages are a purse-style needlebook and a sheath for scissors. Probably early twentieth century. The Merry Cox Collection.*

kept on the person and, in the case of the magnificent embroideries produced by the Japanese, the tools were the property of the family that owned the embroidery business.) Chatelaines in South America were not manufactured but imported by European colonists well into the nineteenth century. Native South Americans did use sewing tools before the time of Christ, but research to this date does not indicate that their container(s) were appended to the waistband or other articles of clothing.

With the decline of the chatelaine's popularity, the individual tools were removed from their chains and incorporated in sewing baskets and workboxes. This obviously accounts for the difficulty in finding complete chatelaines from the antique marketplace, as well as the greater

ease in locating separate tools that seldom appear with any matching pieces. The ardent collector with an abundance of time and funds may accumulate matching appendages, as well as a plaque with its original chains, but the task will demand careful study, and familiarity with jewelers, period designs, and honest, competent dealers. Nevertheless, those who would have a complete collection of needlework tools must indeed own a chatelaine, and the effort to acquire one or many is worthwhile and rewarding.

EDITOR'S NOTE
The chatelaines and appendages pictured with this article are the property of the Needlework Patio of Dallas, Texas; Ann Powell, Ltd., of Stuart, Florida; Merry Cox of Clovis, California; Dawn Lewis of The Needle's Work; Mary Etling Batzel of Arlington, Texas; and the author.

Ann Powell, Ltd., is a purveyor of assorted needlework tools, both old and new, through her catalog. Turn to page 142 for catalog ordering information.

ENDNOTES
[1] *Toys* was a term used for tiny bibelots and whatnots of fine workmanship. A toy shop was very much like the modern, exclusive gift shop.

[2] Genevieve Cummins and Nerylla Taunton, *Chatelaines: Utility to Glorious Extravagance* (Suffolk: Antique Collectors' Club Ltd., 1994), 53.

BIBLIOGRAPHY
Bryk, Nancy., Ed. *American Dress Pattern Catalogs, 1873-1909.* New York: Dover Publications Inc., 1988.

Cummins, Genevieve and Taunton, Nerylla. *Chatelaines: Utility to Glorious Extravagance.* Suffolk: Antique Collectors' Club Ltd., 1994.

Groves, Sylvia. *The History of Needlework Tools and Accessories.* Newton Abbot: David and Charles Ltd., 1973.

Rogers, Gay Ann, *American Silver Thimbles.* London: Haggerston Press, 1989.

---*An Illustrated History of Needlework Tools.* London: John Murray, 1983.

L̲ate-nineteenth-century steel chatelaine with five appendages: thimble bucket, "paper knife," pincushion, needlecase, and tape measure. The "paper knife" may be an instrument used for flattening seams, and would certainly be more appropriate for this distinctly needlework chatelaine; however, such a designation for the tool is not recognized as such by modern researchers. Unmarked, this piece is probably French. The needlecase is not original. The Mary Etling Batzel Collection.

In Search of the Huswif

There is a certain satisfaction achieved when research reveals more than the investigator anticipates. The *huswif* provides a perfect example.

Originally *huswif* was defined as that woman who maintained the order of a house by attending to or directing those activities that assured the satisfactory functioning of the domicile. *Hus* meant *house; wif* meant *woman*. The more modern term, *housewife*, is a derivation of the earlier word and, over time, its definition has become more precise in meaning. By the late eighteenth century, the spelling and significance of the word were the same as those ascribed to it today. However, a variety of spellings was first attributed to the same definition. From *huswif*, also came the word *hussy*, the loose or wanton woman, as well as *hussif, hussive, houswif, housewif,* or *housewife,* all of which meant a "domestic engineer," or a sewing case of some sort or another, and finally, *housewife* even pertained to an oddly tidy fish, which displayed an unusual propensity for mothering her young. *The New Lexicon Webster's Dictionary of the English Language*, Encyclopedic Edition, 1988, still assigns to *housewife*, as a secondary definition peculiar to British English, the common name for "A small case containing pins, needles, thread, etc." The connection is plausible; the container holds, in an orderly fashion, those things necessary for the accomplishment of a task. "A small case" becomes a problem, however, when the material and manner of composition is questioned. Any case of a small size, containing sewing imperatives, might be a housewife. This would explain the housewife appendage mentioned in *The Englishwoman's Domestic Magazine* of late 1873 as a part of a "Housewife's Chatelaine" of "English-made leatherwork . . . holding needles and cotton . . ."[1] as well as the leather-bound, hard-bodied, fitted sewing case illustrated in Gertrude Whiting's *Old-Time Tools & Toys of Needlework* being labeled a housewife.[2]

The *Oxford English Dictionary*, as a tertiary definition, says that a *housewife* is "Usually a pocket-case for needles, pins, thread, scissors, etc.", but in that sense, it is usually spelled *huswife* or *hussive*. In

Late-eighteenth- and nineteenth-century sewing rolls. Also called huswifs, these utilitarian cases, one of which includes a pincushion, are composed mainly of fabric scraps. The two ornate pieces include highly decorative trims. The Examplarery Collection.

addition, the *OED* notes that Laurence Sterne makes reference to the object in *The Life and Opinions of Tristam Shandy, Gentleman* (1762) saying, "To bring whatever he had to say into so small a compass that . . . it might be rolled up in my mother's housewife." And again in *A Sentimental Journey Through France and Italy* (1775), Sterne writes, "(She) without saying a word, took out her little hussive, threaded a small needle, and sewed it up." The housewife was rolled up, indicating a soft body, while the hussive has no such clue-giving description. That Sterne used two different words for the containers of sewing supplies causes one to wonder if, by different spellings, two variations of containers fitted to the same purpose might be unalike in construction or appearance. Upon consideration of a footed container illustrated in Gay Ann Rogers' *An Illustrated History of Needlework Tools* (1983), one becomes convinced that as far back as the eighteenth century, the terms *housewife* and *hussif* were not siblings but cousins. The housewife was actually a long, soft piece of pliable leather or fabric, into which were secured by pinning, tying, or the addition of a small pocket, the necessities of plain work. When the contents were not needed, the material was rolled up and tied closed with ribbons or buttoned closed by button and loop. The hussif was made of a hard substance, metals originally and then celluloid and plastic, and it opened by the separation of two parts that had a screw or friction closure.

The housewife was fashioned commercially and sold by peddlers, as well as proprietors of toy shops.[3] Silk housewives were popular as gifts among young men and women, the former having need of emergency mending tools as much as the latter. The impersonal nature of a housewife made it a socially acceptable gift from a young lady to her beau. Clever needlewomen of all ages also constructed their own housewives; some simply of a length of wide ribbon, others of such fabrics as linen, silken velvets and taffetas, or homespun cotton. Some were embellished with favorite designs, while others served as tiny samplers. Cross-stitched alphabets and motifs, variety and filling stitches, and of course hem and other finishing stitches frequently embellished the tiny sewing servants. The housewife was an ideal project for the schoolgirl beginning her training in work both plain and fancy. Worn under the full skirts or aprons of women or carried in a pocket by men, the housewife supplied mending equipment for those who had left sewing bag or basket behind.

The human housewife gave name to that object which, materially, best defined her person and daily life. Armed with the simplest tools to complete a task, the housewife was and is more than she appears, and is of greater resources than she willingly reveals, especially when research imparts all that she truly is.

ENDNOTES

[1] Genevieve Cummins and Nerylla Taunton, *Chatelaines: Utility to Glorious Extravangance* (Suffolk: Antique Collector's Club Ltd.), 1994.

[2] Gertrude Whiting, *Old-Time Tools & Toys of Needlework* (New York: Dover Publications, Inc.), 1928.

[3] The term *toy* might be better understood today as *trifle*. Shops offering small and unusual merchandise were especially popular during the rise of Britain's merchant class, when new money was displayed by the possession of fine baubles and clever contraptions. They were called toy shops not because the offerings were like a child's playthings, but because they were diminutive. The term is an ancestor of today's *toy*; another example of word specialization.

Late-Twentieth-Century Huswif

Fashioned after a piece housed in the Victoria and Albert Museum in London, England, this decorative huswif, or sewing and thread case, can be used by the modern-day needlewoman as a treasured tool carrier that possesses significant ties to our needleworking past. Some sources have indicated that huswifs were popular projects in charity schools during the 1700s and early 1800s in Britain. In addition, it has been stated that these little folding bags, which contained all the basic necessities for sewing and mending, were issued to all soldiers and sailors in Britain. The pieces got their names from the fact that they acted in the place of a housewife. This design features three solidly stitched pockets in which to house needleworking and sewing tools and accessories. In addition, vignettes inspired by antique needlework adorn the reverse side. The huswif folds to fit inside a carrying case that is embellished with a

house, a ship, and a border motif that is reminiscent of ocean waves. Notice that the ship's bow is pointing toward home; symbolism indicating a wish for a safe return. For more information about huswifs, refer to *In Search of the Huswif* on page 63.

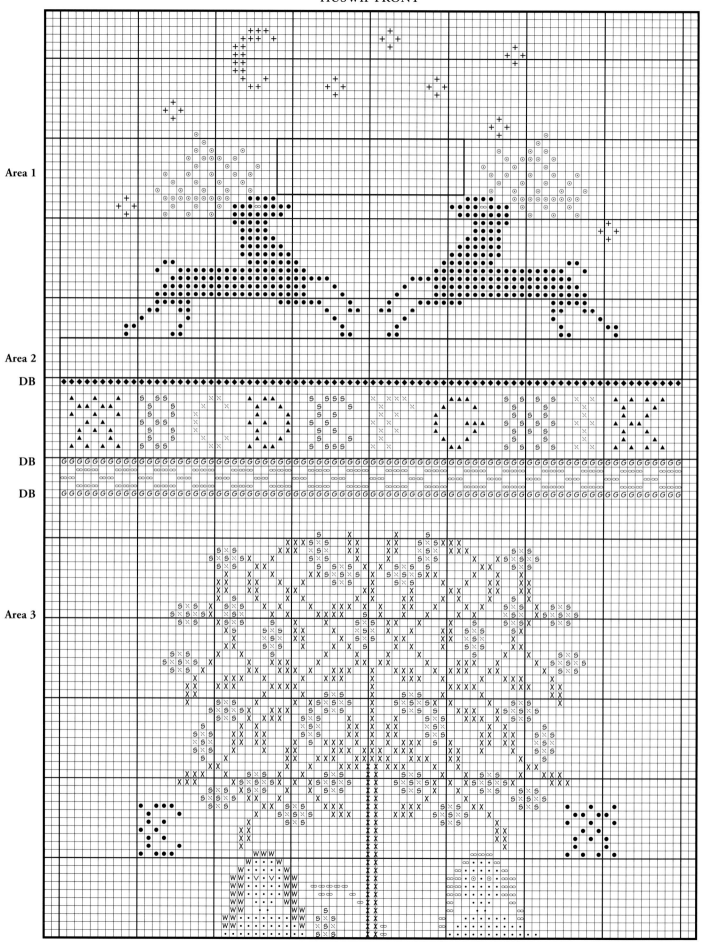

Shaded portion indicates overlap from previous page.

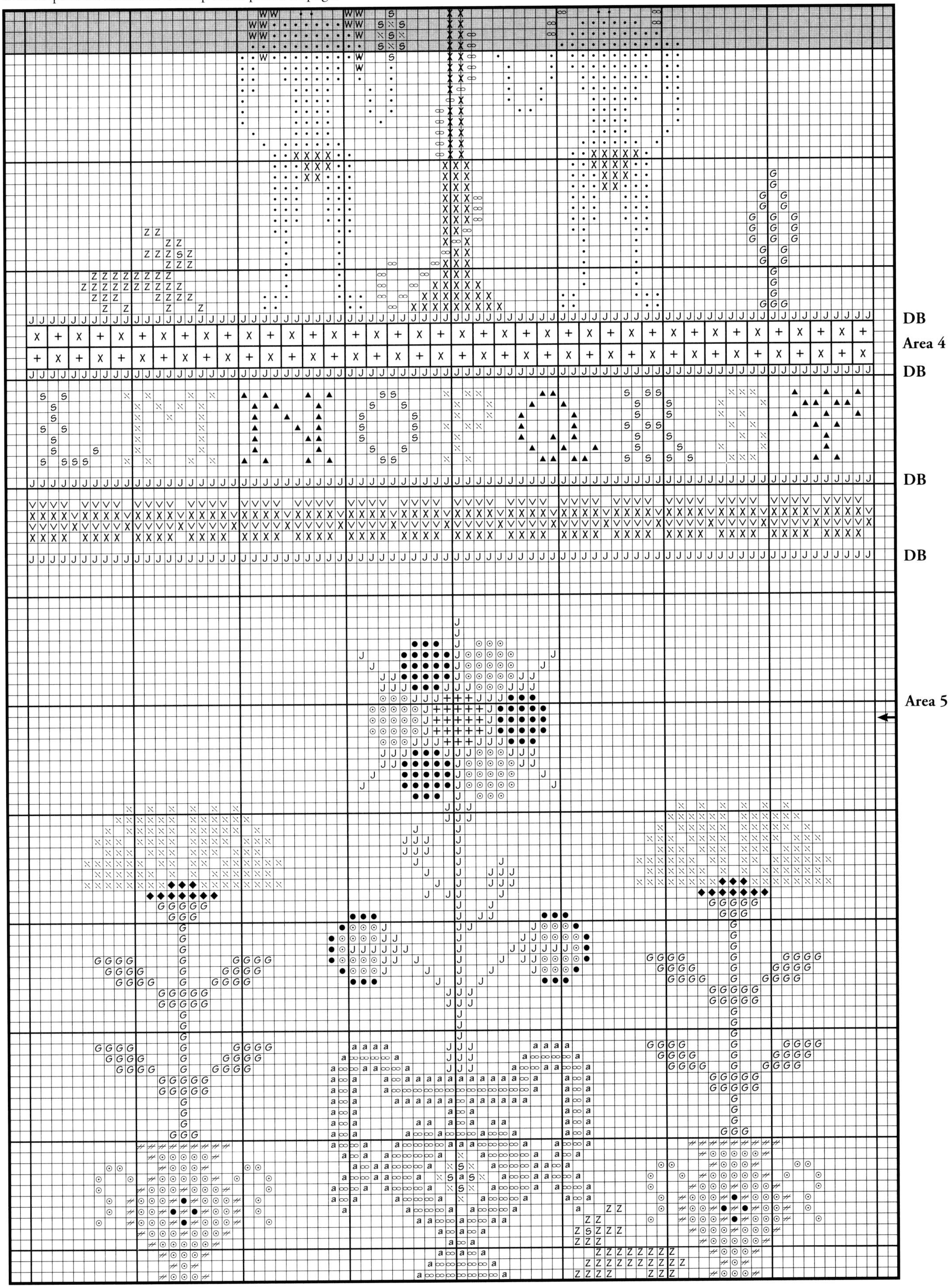

DB

Area 4

DB

DB

DB

Area 5

Shaded portion indicates overlap from previous page.

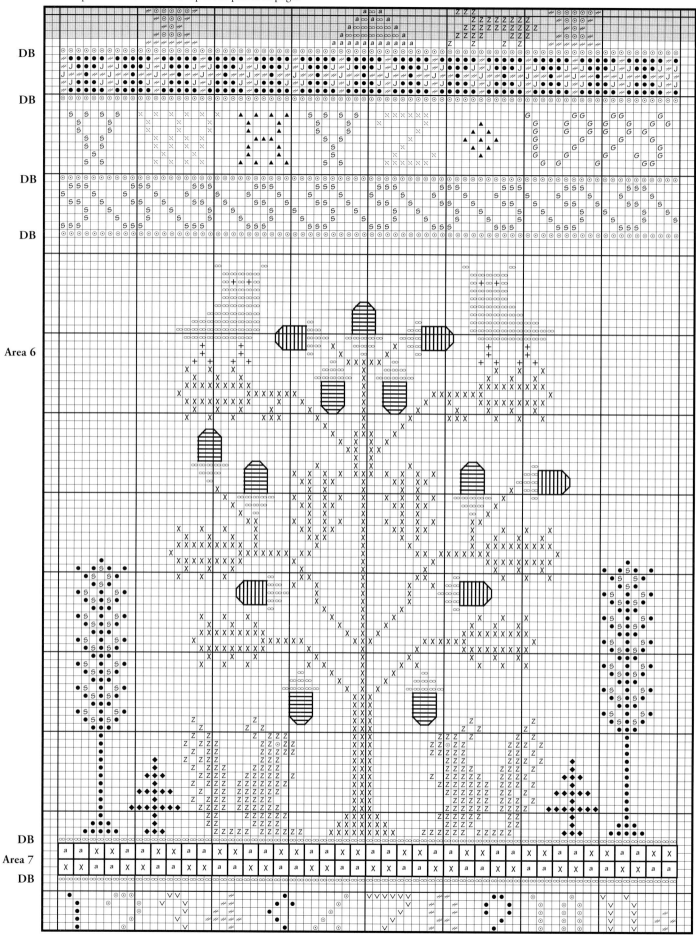

DB
DB
DB
DB
Area 6
DB
Area 7
DB

68

Shaded portion indicates overlap from previous page.

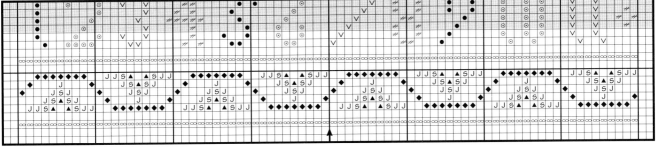

DB

Area 8

DB

Late-Twentieth-Century Huswif

	DMC	Kreinik FT	Soie d'Alger	
X	3362	2937	3726	pine green, dk.
J	3363	2469	3723	pine green, med.
◆	500	2500	1846	blue-green, vy. dk.
G	501	2501	1844	blue-green, dk.
●	924	2924	206	gray-green, vy. dk.
⊙	3768	2768	1746	gray-green, dk.
v	926	2926	1745	gray-green, dk.
#	927	2927	1744	gray-green, med.
▲	3777	2354	2636	terra cotta, vy. dk.
S	3830	2354	2636	terra cotta
✕	3778	2356	2914	terra cotta, lt.
W	433	2433	4116	brown, med.
∞	420	2782	3816	hazelnut, dk.
a	422	2673	3812	hazelnut, lt.
+	3828	—	—	hazelnut
Z	3790	2609	3344	beige-gray, ul. dk.
•	407	2407	4611	flesh, dk.
£	3779	2759	2912	terra cotta, ul. vy. lt.
	502	2502	—	blue-green

Fabric: 36-count tea-dyed Irish linen from Charles Craft, Inc. (**NOTE:** Cut one piece of fabric 25½" x 16" for front and back of huswif. Cut two fabric pieces **each** 19½" x 12" for case. One piece will be used for stitching design; the other for finishing. Cut three fabric pieces **each** 9½" square for back panel pockets.)

Stitch count:
Huswif front and back	351H x 80W
Queen-Stitch Pocket	48H x 84W
Irish-Stitch Pocket	50H x 82W
Rice-Stitch Pocket	48H x 82W
Case	208H x 127W

Design size:
Huswif
28-count	25" x 5¾"
30-count	23⅜" x 5⅜"
32-count	22" x 5"
36-count	19½" x 4½"

Case
28-count	14⅞" x 9"
30-count	13⅞" x 8½"
32-count	13" x 8"
36-count	11½" x 7¼"

NOTE: Please read instructions carefully before beginning. To match front and back of huswif, stitch the front and back side by side, 1" apart, on the same piece of fabric. Align the first dividing band on the front with the first dividing band on Area 1 of the back. Areas 2, 3, and 4 on the back are stitched on separate pieces of fabric and attached as pockets.

Instructions: Cross stitch over two threads, using two strands of floss.

Special instructions:
Dividing Bands (DB): Work double backstitch for all dividing bands, using two strands of floss.

Huswif front
Area 1: Cross stitch initials using sampler alphabet.
Area 2: Work Irish stitch using two strands 500/2500/1846 where █ appears, 501/2501/1844 where ▌ appears, and 502/2502/— where ▏ appears. Beginning in center of stitching area, work design as shown in Area 2 Illustration—Irish Stitch, repeating boxed areas twice more to right and left.
Area 3: Work rice stitch over two threads for fruit on tree and in Eve's hand, using one strand of floss.
Area 4: Work rice stitch over four threads, using two strands of floss.
Area 5: Work arrowhead stitch in center of center flower where symbol + appears, using one strand of floss.
Area 6: Work satin stitch for acorns, using two strands 422/2673/3812 and stitching in direction indicated by lines on chart.

Area 7: Work Algerian eye stitch using two strands of floss.
Area 8: Work Smyrna cross stitch in center of each flower where symbol ▲ appears, using two strands of floss.

Huswif back
Work eyelet stitch over six threads for center of flowers, using two strands of floss. Cross stitch initials using sampler alphabet, centering initials within boxed areas. Work rice stitch over four threads between dividing bands, using two strands of floss. Repeat this dividing-band section at bottom of huswif back, aligning bottom dividing band with last dividing band of front.

69

NOTE: For all back-panel pockets, stitch charted design on top half of linen piece.

Queen-Stitch Pocket: Work clusters of four queen stitches where indicated on chart by diamond-shaped boxes, using two strands of floss. Work half queen stitches along edges. Work diagonal double backstitch around queen stitches, using two strands of floss and referring to Queen-Stitch Pocket Illustration.

Irish-Stitch Pocket: Work Irish stitch using two strands of floss.

	1	**2**	**3**	**4**
▬▬	3362	3777	420	924
▭	3363	3830	3828	3768
▭	422	422	422	422
▭	3828	3828	3828	3828

NOTE: Outer border of Irish-Stitch Pocket Illustration—Detail is indicated by dark, vertical lines on Irish-Stitch Pocket chart.

Rice-Stitch Pocket: Work rice stitch over four threads, using two strands of floss.

Huswif case

Area 1: Work satin stitch for acorn, using two strands 422/2673/3812.

Area 2: Personalize using sampler alphabet.

Area 3: Work Algerian eye stitch over four threads for border under name and over six threads for centers of stars, using two strands of floss.

House: Work double backstitch for roof and grass, using two strands of floss. Work rice stitch over two threads for windowpanes, using one strand of floss. Backstitch windowpanes using one strand 422/2673/3812. Backstitch door using one strand 3790/2609/3344.

Ship rigging: Work diagonal straight stitches using one strand 3790/2609/3344, referring to Illustration A on page 78. Weave horizontal straight stitches through diagonal straight stitches. Work long stitches for rigging, using one strand 3790/2609/3344 and referring to Illustration B on page 79. Couch long stitches in place.

Finishing instructions:
Materials:

Two 6½" x 4⅜" pieces tan lightweight worsted-wool fabric (for holding needles)

15" x 8" piece interfacing (for case)

2 yds. 1"-wide dark green worsted-wool binding

Thread to match binding

Thread to match linen

Hand-sewing needle

Straight pins (**NOTE:** Non-plastic-head pins will work best for this project, due to the heat of the iron required to press wool.)

Scissors Pencil

Iron and press cloth

Sewing machine with zipper foot (optional) (**NOTE:** Zipper foot will be handy for attaching stitched panel pockets to back side of huswif.)

NOTE: Binding for this project was custom-dyed to match floss. For ordering information, turn to page 142.

Late-Twentieth-Century Huswif

1. Complete stitching following instructions given.

2. Work blanket or buttonhole stitch around perimeter of each piece of worsted-wool fabric, using two strands DMC FT 2890. Layer two pieces of wool, aligning lengthwise edges but staggering short edges at one end ⅝". Pin. Measure up 3½" from shortest short edge and mark. Sew wool pieces together along marking, and remove pins. Place assembled wool pieces atop back side of huswif, with stitching line ¼" below bottom of top dividing band. Pin and then sew in place, using previous stitching line as a guide for sewing. Set aside.

3. Lightly mark ⅛"–¼" up from top of bottom dividing band, marking along track of fabric to achieve a straight line. Pin rice-stitch pocket to right side of fabric on back side of huswif, pinning along marking and aligning bottom edge of stitching with marking. (**NOTE:** Wrong side of stitched pocket will be facing up, and will be below the marking.) Sew pocket to back of huswif along edge of stitching.

NOTE: If using sewing machine, use zipper foot to get as close as possible to edge of stitching.

4. Fold stitched portion of rice-stitch pocket toward top of huswif, using sewing line as a fold line and aligning edge of pocket stitching with edge of dividing-band stitching along sides. Pin in place, and press pocket, using a press cloth so as not to flatten stitches. Cut 5"-long piece from binding. Fold in half

along lengthwise edge and press. Remove pins from pocket as needed, and hand sew binding to top, lengthwise, raw edges of pocket. Replace pins to hold pocket flat against huswif fabric.

5. Repeat for Irish-stitch pocket and then for queen-stitch pocket, placing bottom edge of each pocket ¾" above top, bound edge of each previous pocket. Remove pins.

6. Lightly mark a vertical line halfway between front and back stitching, marking along track of fabric to achieve a straight line. Fold fabric at mark. Press along edge of fabric to crease, being careful not to flatten stitches. Pin fabric layers together in several places to secure. Pin pattern to fabric, aligning stitching line on pattern with edge of stitching along sides. (**NOTE:** Ends of pattern lines should be aligned with bottom of top dividing band on huswif back.) Trace around pattern to mark curve, and remove pattern. Sew bottom, side, top curve, and remaining side to secure huswif front and back, sewing in seam-allowance area.

7. Blind stitch binding around perimeter of huswif, using thread to match binding.

Case

1. Complete stitching following instructions given.

2. Center *Case* pattern atop stitched, case exterior. (**NOTE:** Pattern does not include seam allowance: leave excess fabric for seam allowance when cutting. Lightly mark pattern ends on fabric to indicate location of top of case opening. Extend pattern 9⅜" from ends shown.) Trace lightly around entire pattern, drawing a straight line across bottom edge. Remove pattern. Repeat on unstitched piece of linen and on interfacing.

3. Pin stitched piece of linen and interfacing together, placing interfacing atop wrong side of stitched piece, aligning edges, and sewing around perimeter ¼" in from edge. Place assembled interfacing and stitched piece interfacing-side down atop a flat surface. Place unstitched piece of linen (lining) atop assembled piece and pin to secure. Hand or machine sew around edges, using a ½" seam allowance and leaving an opening for turning.

4. Trim seams, clip curves, and turn right-side out. Press. Blind stitch opening

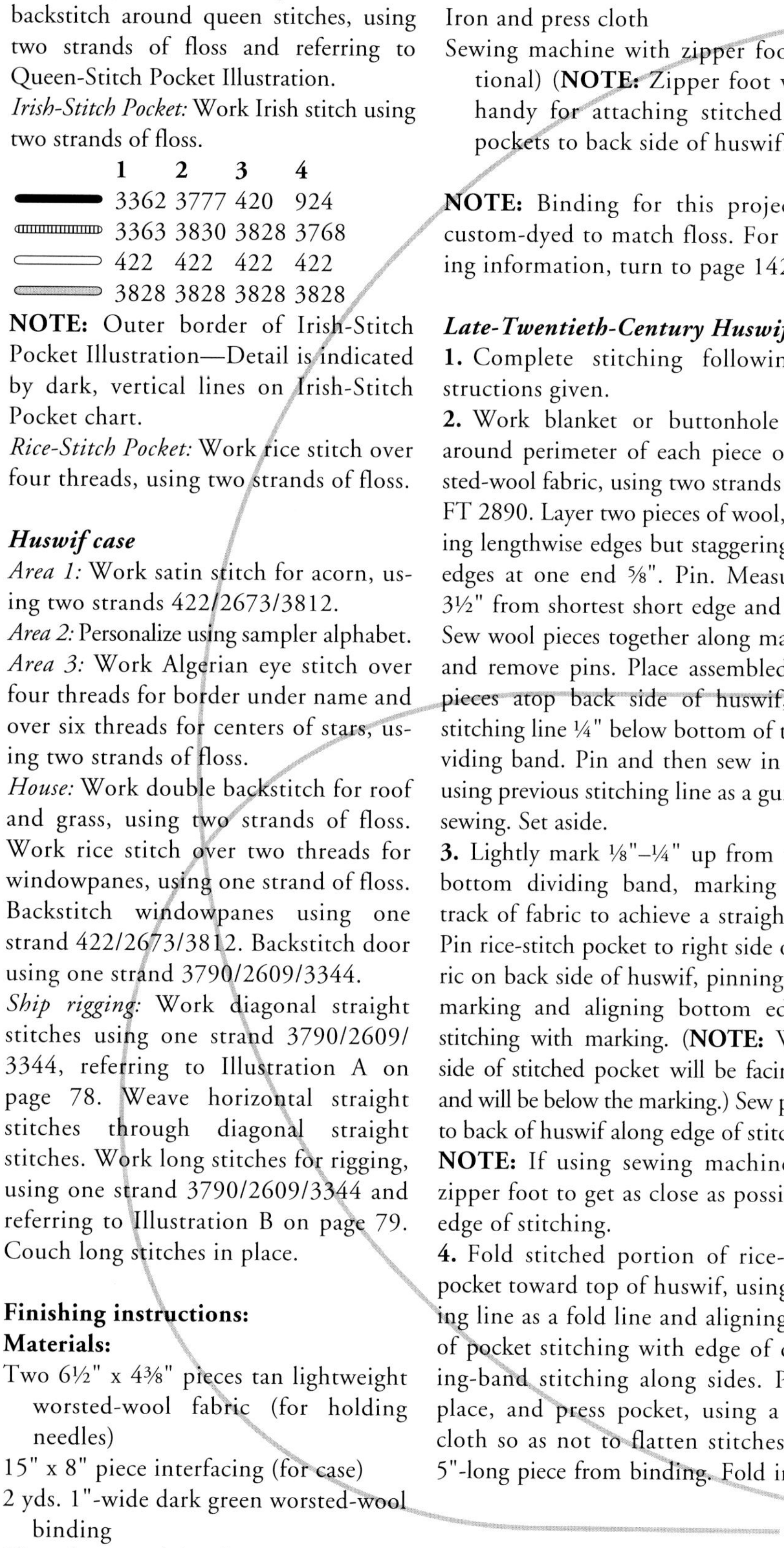

Huswif Pattern

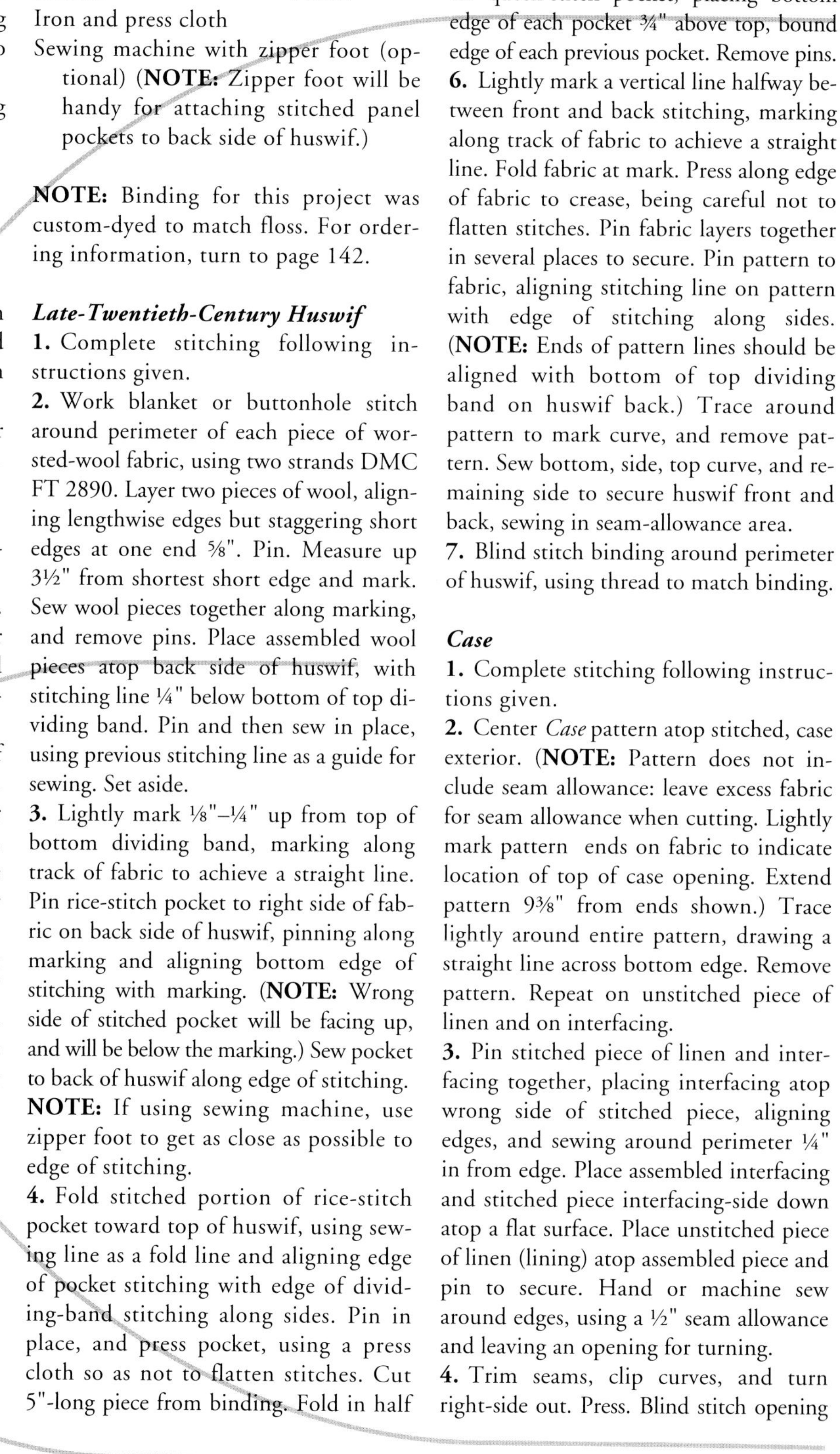

Case Pattern

closed, using thread to match linen.

5. Place case stitched-side up atop a flat surface. Fold case under ⅛" below bottom of wave border that is stitched below house and ship, aligning left and right edges of case. Press to crease bottom of case. Turn case over, and whipstitch case edges together on left and right sides, using thread to match fabric. Turn case over again, and fold case flap under ⅛" above top of wave border at top of house and ship design. Press to crease top of case.

NOTE: We did not include a closure on the case. If desired, include a closure of your choosing, or simply tie a complementary length of ribbon around entire case to hold flap closed.

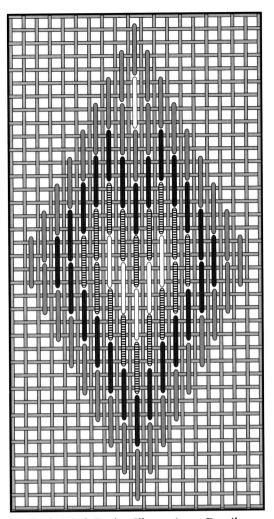

Irish-Stitch Pocket Illustration—Detail

Queen-Stitch Pocket Illustration

TOP

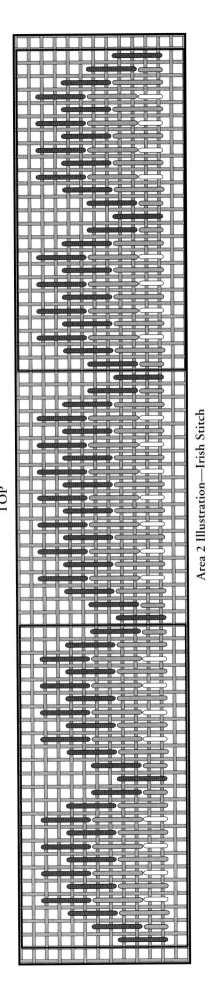

Area 2 Illustration—Irish Stitch

LATE-TWENTIETH-CENTURY HUSWIF BACK

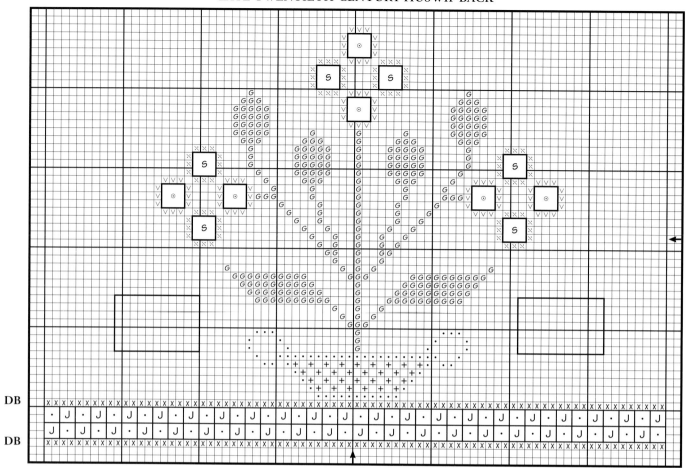

QUEEN-STITCH POCKET

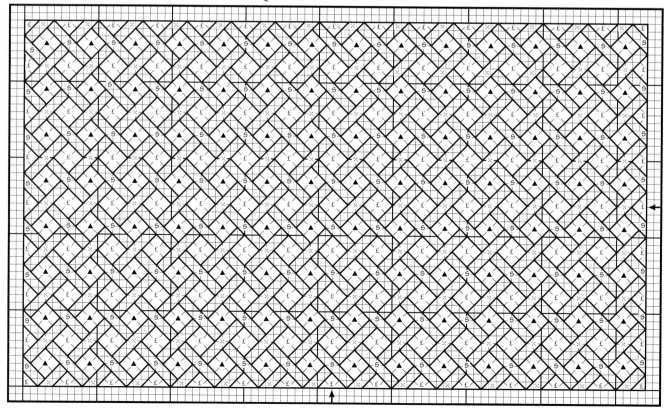

IRISH-STITCH POCKET

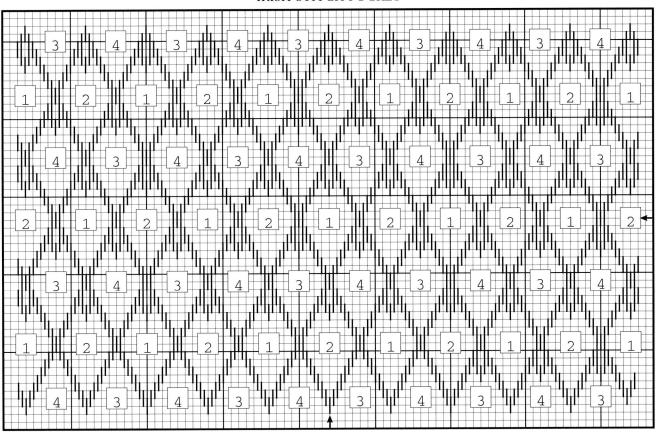

RICE-STITCH POCKET

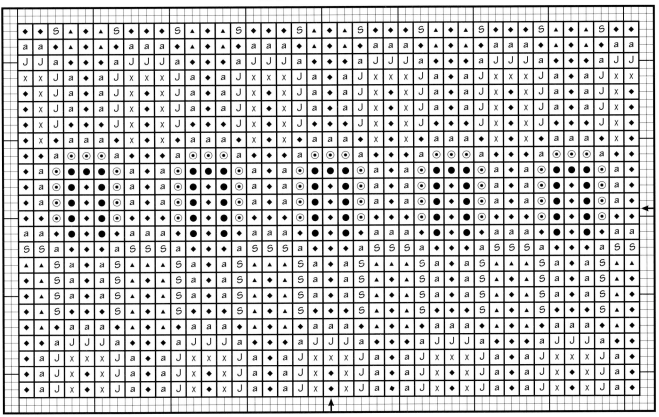

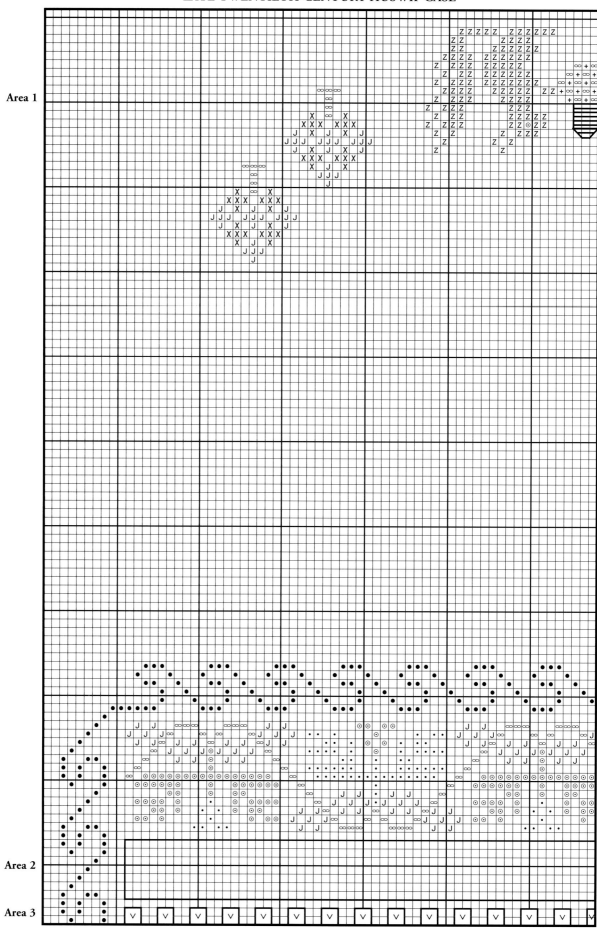

Area 1

Area 2

Area 3

Shaded portion indicates overlap from previous page.

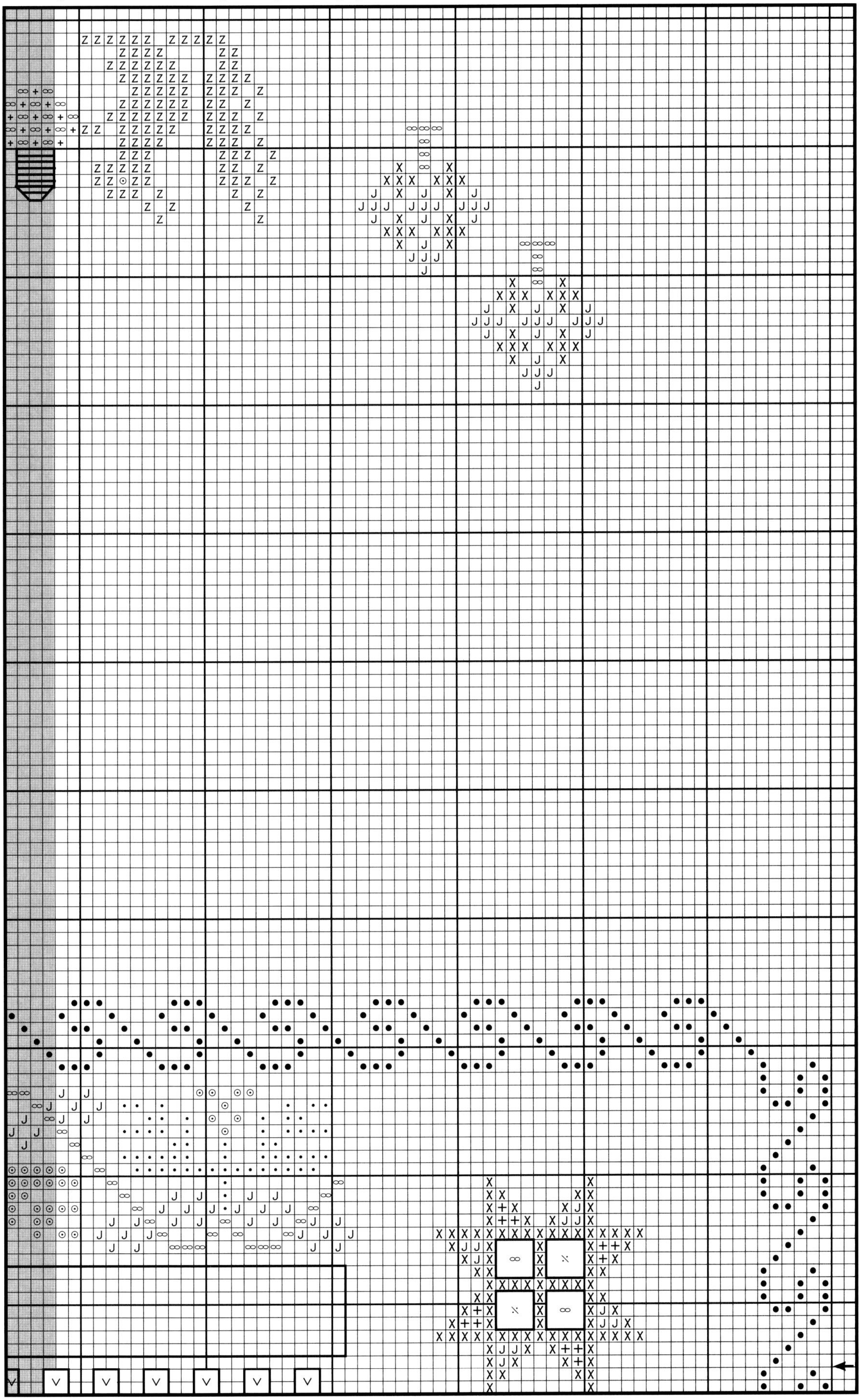

Area 3

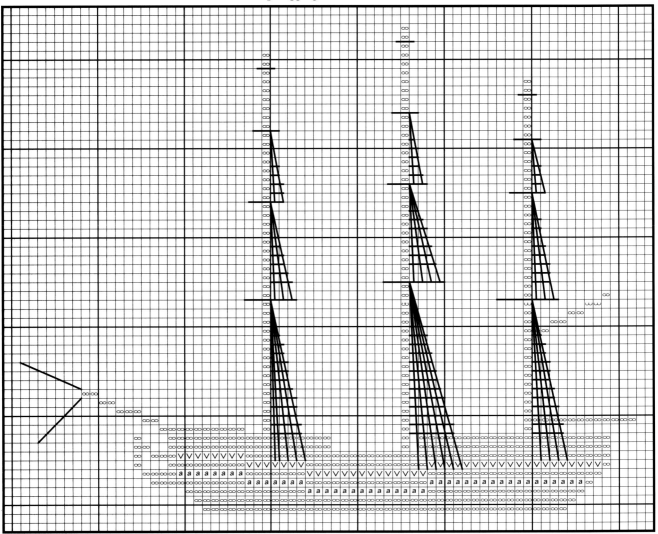

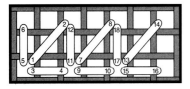

Arrowhead Stitch

Rice Stitch
(Over 4)

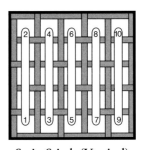

Satin Stitch (Vertical)

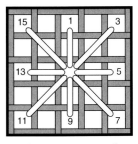

Algerian Eye Stitch

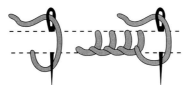

Buttonhole Stitch

Rice Stitch
(Over 2)

Smyrna Cross
(Over 2)

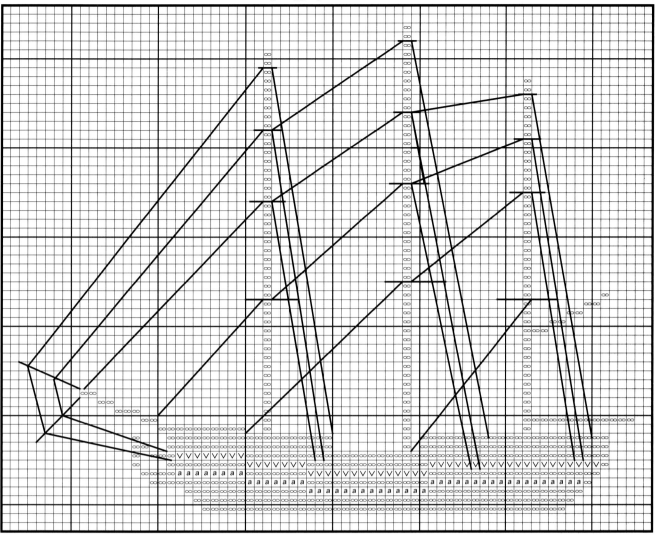

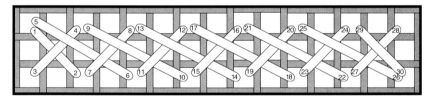

Double Backstitch

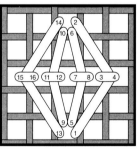

Queen Stitch

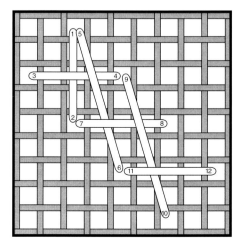

Diagonal Double Backstitch

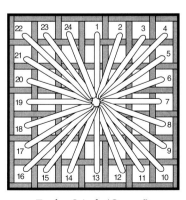

Eyelet Stitch (Over 6)

Guide My Heart Sampler

This vibrant and intriguing design possesses influences from samplers of days gone by, presented in a modern-day format that is very pleasing. The central focus is a wide, meandering, floral band that is distinctly reminiscent of seventeenth-century English samplers. Worked predominantly in cross stitch, this piece also includes four-sided, satin, Montenegrin, and Algerian eye stitches, as well as sections of cross stitch worked over one thread. Comprised of alphabets, numerals, multiple rows of interesting dividing bands, and a pious verse—further inspiration from pieces of the past—this eye-catching sampler is completed by a colorful border of leaves and berries. Ideal for the needleworker who has mastered cross stitch and is ready to begin learning new skills, this delightful piece will provide a wonderful opportunity to add mastery of additional stitches to one's repertoire while creating a beautiful decorative piece for the home.

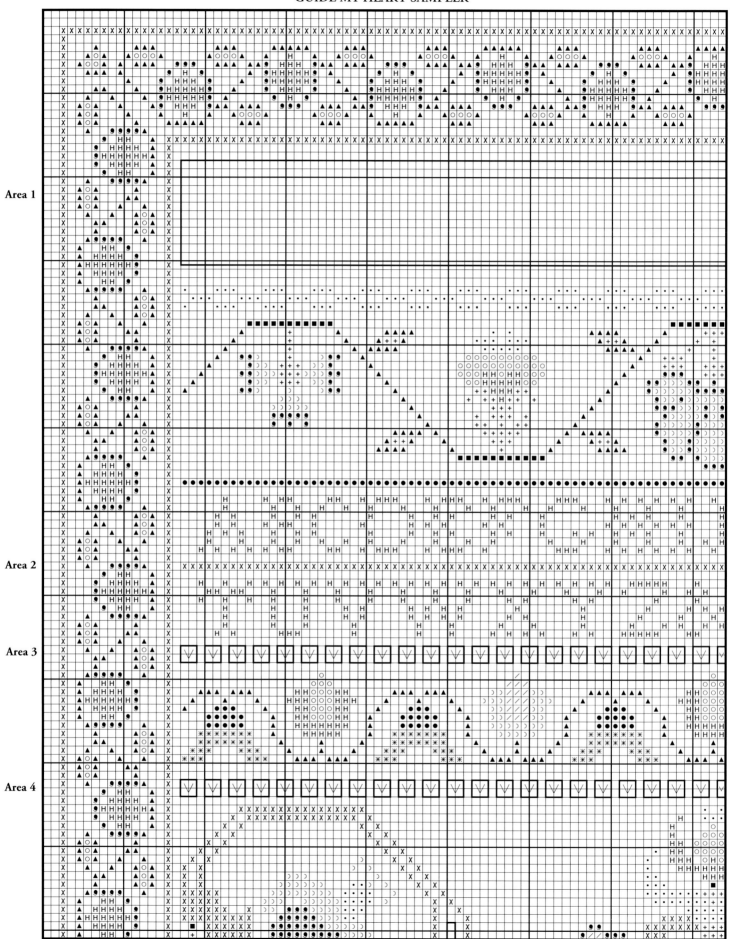

Shaded portion indicates overlap from previous page.

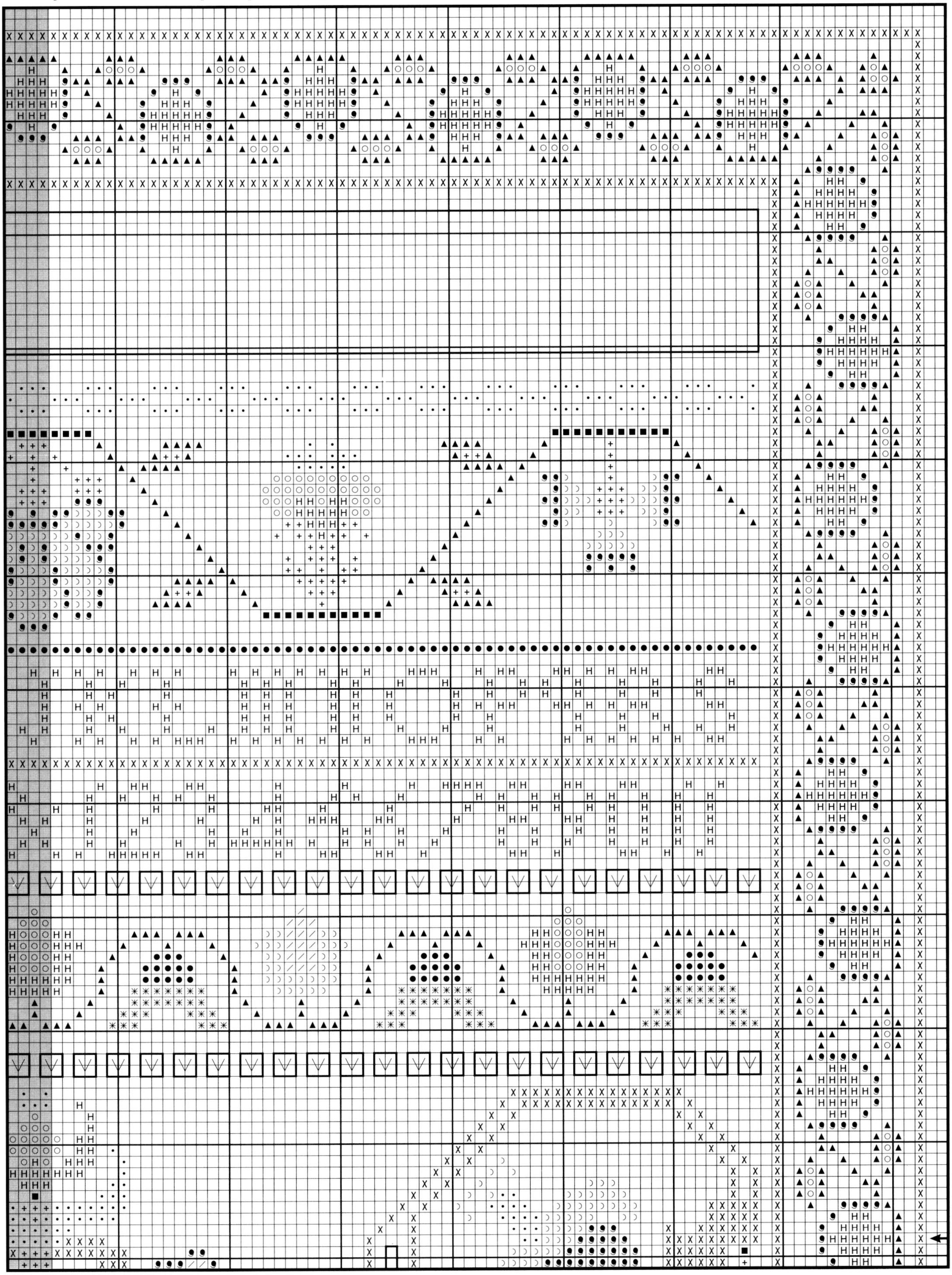

Shaded portion indicates overlap from page 82.

Area 5

Area 6

Area 7

Area 8

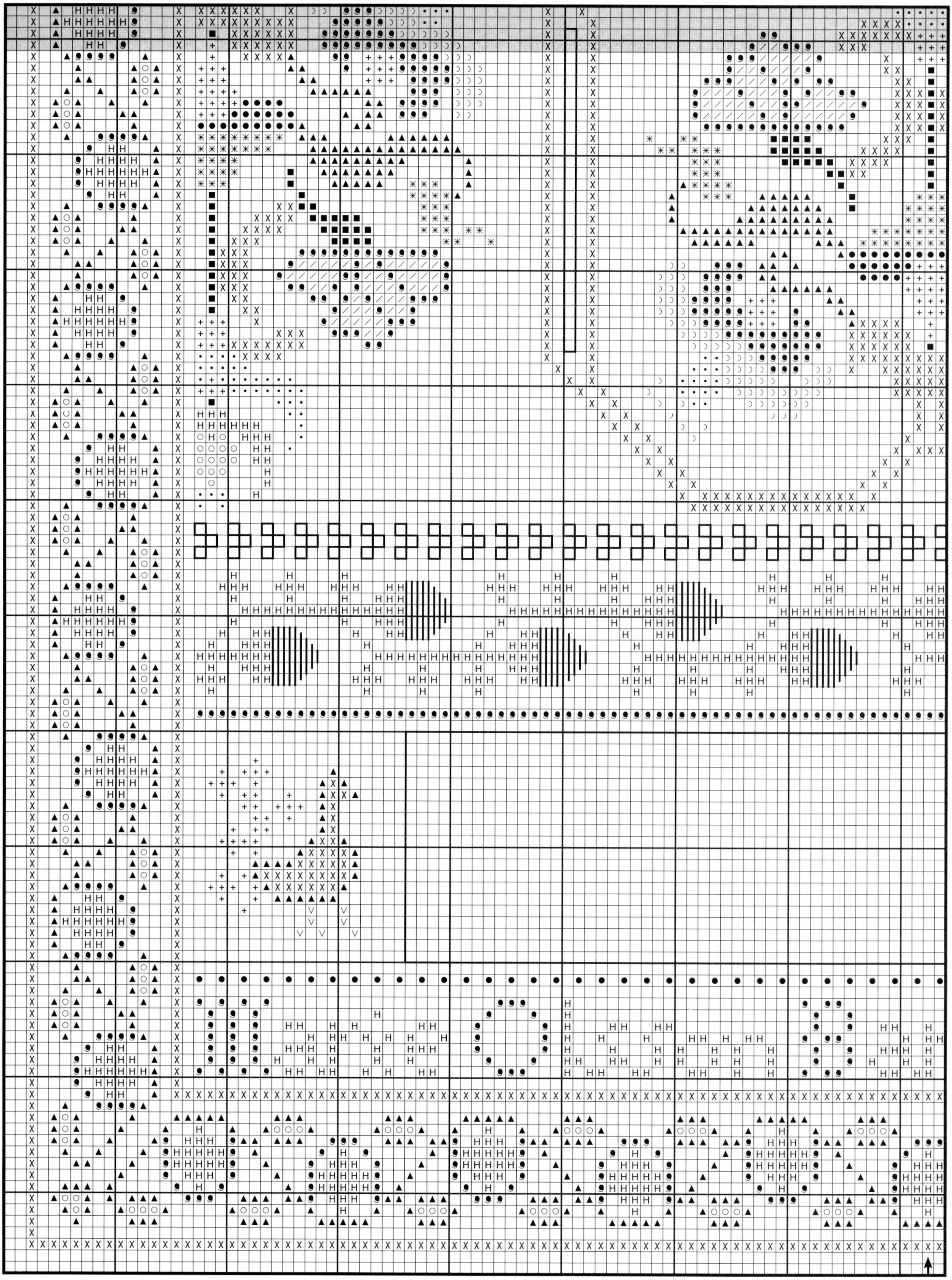

Shaded portion indicates overlap from previous page and page 83.

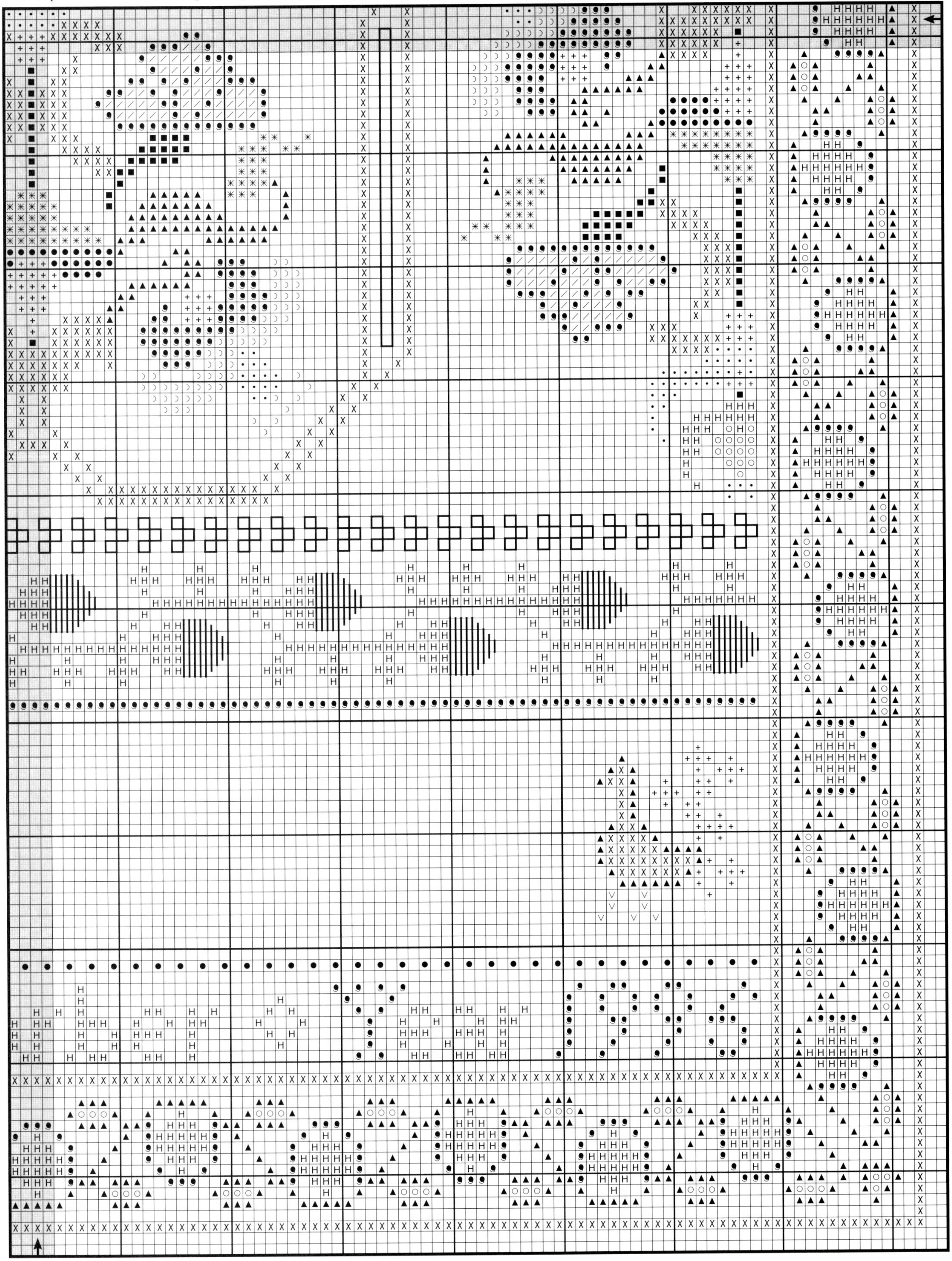

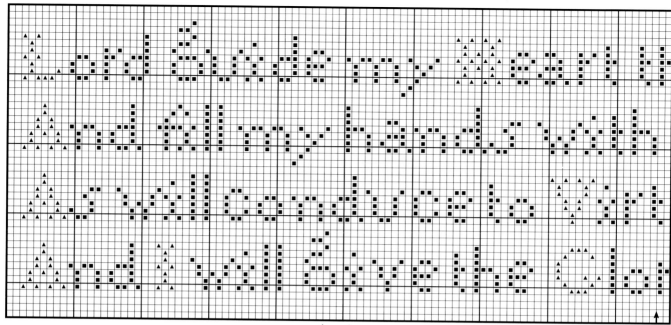

Area 8

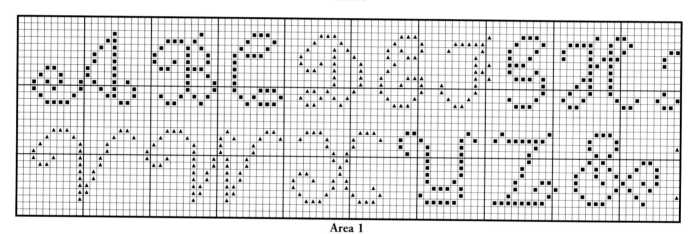

Area 1

Guide My Heart Sampler

DMC	Kreinik DMC FT	Soie d'Alger	
X 502	2502	1843	blue-green
▲ 501	2501	3426	blue-green, dk.
● 930	2930	1736	antique blue, dk.
○ 676	2673	2242	old gold, lt.
⊃ 356	2356	4612	terra cotta, med.
◑ 3777	2354	2636	terra cotta, vy. dk.
/ 754	2754	2912	peach flesh, lt.
+ 368	2369	1842	pistachio, lt.
✳ 3755	2325	112	baby blue
• ecru	ecru	F2	ecru
v 3782	2611	—	mocha brown, lt.
H 436	2436	4235	tan
■ 3750	2929	1716	antique blue, vy. dk.

Fabric: 32-count parchment Jobelan from Wichelt Imports, Inc.
Stitch count: 213H x 161W

Design size:

25-count	17" x 12⅞"
28-count	15¼" x 11½"
32-count	13⅜" x 10"
36-count	11⅞" x 9"

Instructions: Cross stitch over two threads, using two strands of floss unless otherwise indicated.

Special instructions:
Areas 1 & 8: Cross stitch over one thread, using one strand of floss.

Area 2: Work Montenegrin stitch using two strands of floss.

Areas 3 & 4: Work Algerian eye stitch using two strands of floss.

Area 5: Work double backstitch vertically in center of stems, using two strands 3782/2611/—.

Area 6: Work four-sided stitch using one strand 930/2930/1736.

Area 7: Work satin stitch for flower buds, using two strands 676/2673/2242.

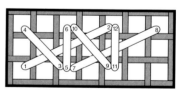

Montenegrin Stitch

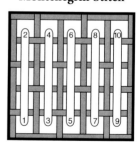

Satin Stitch (Vertical)

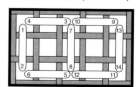

Four-Sided Stitch

Shaded portion indicates overlap from previous page.

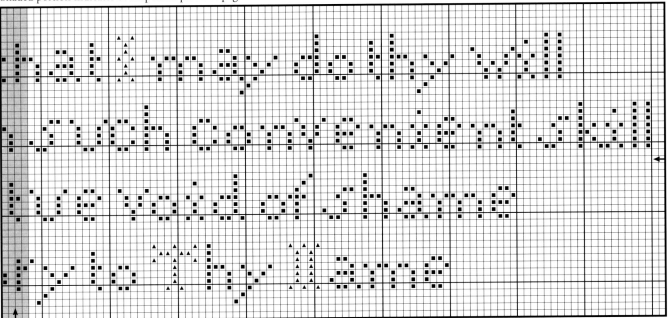

Shaded portion indicates overlap from previous page.

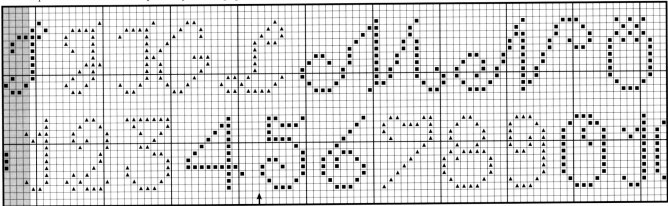

Shaded portion indicates overlap from chart above.

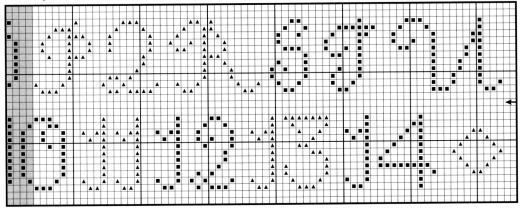

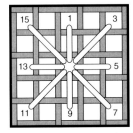

Algerian Eye Stitch

Double Backstitch

ELEGANCE IN WHITE

Whitework Duet

Beautiful, white-on-white stitchery, combined with clever finishing techniques, transforms this pair of designs into pieces that are certain to be admired, whether they are put to use in their maker's home or given as gifts to treasured friends who share a passion for exquisite needlework. The bookmark will be ideal for holding one's place while reading, perhaps, about antique needlework and its history. The pin-pillow top was sewn atop a light blue pin pillow; each stitcher can determine the color she prefers based on the colors used to decorate her home, or on those of other needleworking and sewing implements in her collection. The versatile pin-pillow top has the added benefit of being used as a serviette—the designer's intended use for her creation.

This pair of related designs features the stunning elegance of white-on-white stitchery. Presented in a duet of utilitarian pieces that will delight needle mavins and book enthusiasts alike, these pieces have the added benefit of being completed quickly, making them ideal for gift giving.

90

Pulled-Thread Bookmark

DMC Pearl Cotton (Coton Perlé)
#8 white
#5 white

Fabric: 30-count white linen (**NOTE:** Cut fabric 10" x 5".)
Stitch count: 199H x 69W
Design size:

25-count	8" x 2¾"
27-count	7⅜" x 2½"
30-count	6⅝" x 2¼"
32-count	6¼" x 2⅛"

NOTE: Grid lines on chart represent weave of linen.

Instructions: Work all stitches using one strand of pearl cotton. Use #22 tapestry needle with #5 pearl cotton and #24 tapestry needle with #8 pearl cotton.

Special instructions:

Inner border: Work cable stitch using DMC #5 pearl cotton, referring to Cable Stitch Instructions and Illustrations.

Area 1: Work straight stitches in direction indicated by arrows to form veins of holly leaves, using DMC #8 pearl cotton. Work raised needleweaving through the veins. Refer to Needlewoven Holly Leaves Instructions and Illustrations.

NOTE: Cut a 36" length of pearl cotton in order to work the entire stitch with a single length.

Area 2: Work Greek cross stitch using DMC #8 pearl cotton, referring to Greek Cross Stitch Instructions and Illustrations. Backstitch initial over two threads in center of Greek-cross-stitch area, using DMC #8 pearl cotton and alphabet provided.

Outer border: Backstitch outer edge over four threads, using DMC #8 pearl cotton and pulling stitches gently. Fold edges of fabric back along backstitching and work Nun's stitch through both thicknesses, using DMC #8 pearl cotton. Refer to Finishing Instructions and Illustrations.

Cable Stitch Instructions

Count in one and one-half inches from left edge of fabric and down from top to locate starting point. Begin working cable stitches, bringing needle up at 1 and going down at arrow. Cross two fabric threads to the left, go up two fabric threads, and bring needle up at 2 and down at arrow. See Illustration 1. Cross two fabric threads to the right, go up two fabric threads, and bring needle up at 3 and down at arrow. Continue in this manner, following chart and working cable stitches to complete inner border. Note the change in pattern when turning corners. See Illustration 2.

Needlewoven Holly Leaves Instructions

From the bottom of the fifth, inside cable stitch on the left side, count to the right nineteen threads. This is point A. Bring needle up at point A to begin laying the threads to form the veins of the holly leaves. See Illustration 3. Count to the left ten threads and go down at arrow 1. Bring needle up from back side of fabric at point A, and go down at arrow 2. Continue forming veins in this manner, referring to Illustration 3. After the ninth vein has been completed, bring needle up at point A. The remainder of the leaf will be

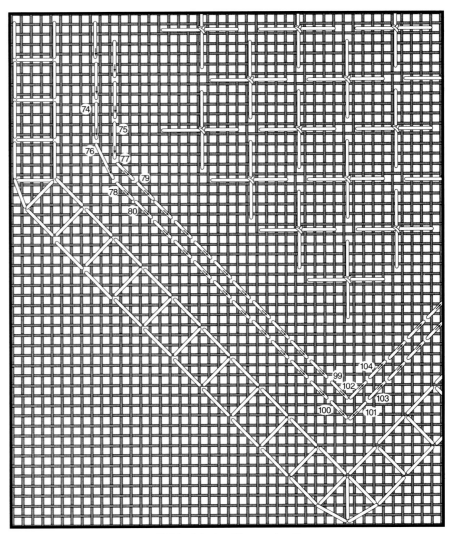

Cable Stitch—Illustration 1

Cable Stitch—Illustration 2

91

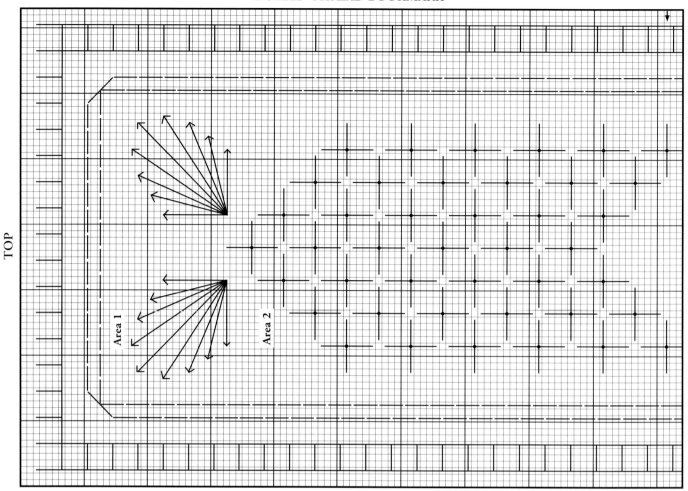

worked atop the surface, without piercing the fabric. Run needle over vein one, under vein two, over vein three, under vein four, etc., until you reach the ninth vein. See Illustration 3. Tighten the stitches, being careful not to distort the veins, and pack the stitches to the bottom of the leaf. Work the second row of needleweaving opposite the first, going under vein nine, over vein eight, etc. Continue in this manner until all veins are full, dropping the shorter veins as you go. When all

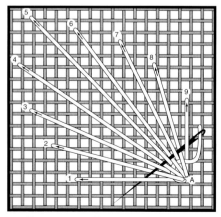

Needlewoven Holly Leaves—Illustration 3

veins are packed, cross the center vein, go down through the fabric, and run the thread under the veins on the back to tie off. Work another holly leaf, a mirror image of the first, with point A being ten threads to the right of point A on the first holly leaf.

Greek Cross Stitch Instructions

From the center point between the base of the holly leaves, count down eight threads and bring needle up at this point. This is point 1 on Illustration 4. Turn fabric ninety degrees clockwise and work the first Greek cross stitch by bringing needle up at point 1 and down at point 2, leaving a loop of thread. Bring needle up four threads to the right of point 1 and four threads below point 2 to establish center of stitch, placing tip of needle over loop of thread. Pull at this point to compress threads. Again, holding a loop of thread, go down at point 3, bring needle up at center, and place tip of needle over loop of thread. Pull. Go down at point 4, holding a loop of thread, come up in the center, and place tip of needle over loop

of thread. Pull. Cross over the center to the opposite side and go back down in the center to complete the stitch.

NOTE: To achieve the pulled, lacy appearance, you must cross the back of the area where the next stitch will be placed. Rows are worked diagonally. See Illustration 5.

NOTE: Illustration 5 shows rows of three Greek cross stitches. The number of stitches worked per row on this project will vary. Illustration is included as an indication of the journey from one diagonal row to the next.

Finishing Instructions

Count out from top, left cable stitch (labeled stitch 2 in Illustration 1) eight threads and up eight threads. Begin working backstitches over four threads, pulling each stitch gently to compress the fabric threads together. (**NOTE:** Read chart carefully when turning corners; these stitches are not uniform. Do not work backstitches across the top.) Crease the left side along backstitching. Begin working Nun's stitch at the top, left cor-

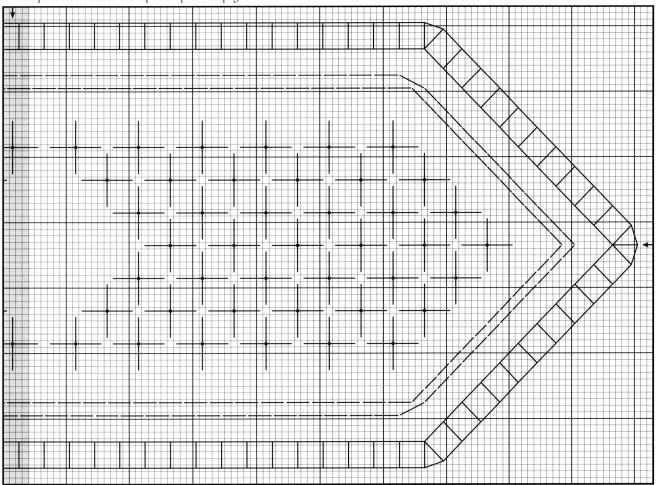

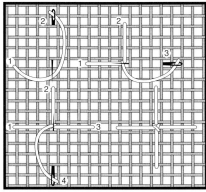

Greek Cross Stitch—Illustration 4

ner through both thicknesses of fabric, referring to Illustration 6. Bring needle up at point 1, and go down at point 2. Bring needle up again at point 1 and down again at point 2. Pull thread gently to compress the fabric threads. Bring needle up at point 3 and down at point 4. Bring needle up again at point 3 and down again at point 4. Continue this pattern to the stitch just before the turn. At this point, gently fold fabric along backstitching to work diagonal Nun's

stitch. Work down to the next-to-last stitch before the point. Again, gently fold fabric along backstitching on diagonal to work diagonal Nun's stitch coming up the lower-right side. Again, work to the next-to-last stitch on the diagonal, and fold fabric along backstitching to work up the right side. Work to the top, turn, and work across the top without creasing the fabric, stitching through a single thickness of fabric, except at edges, where previous folds are located.

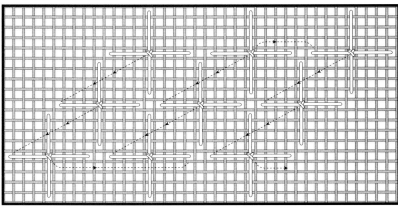

Greek Cross Stitch—Illustration 5

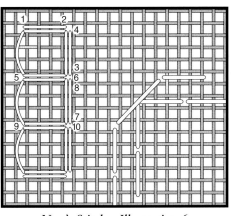

Nun's Stitch—Illustration 6

To fringe, remove the horizontal threads across the top above the Nun's stitches. Tack tassel at bottom point, using complementary sewing thread.

Tassel-Making Instructions:
Wrap fibers around 1½"-long piece of sturdy cardboard to desired thickness, referring to Step 1. Slip tie under cardboard at top of tassel; tie tightly. See Step 2. Remove from cardboard. Wrap second thread around neck of tassel. See Step 3. Wrap thread tails around tie, referring to Step 4, and bury end in tassel. Cut along bottom of tassel through all fibers.

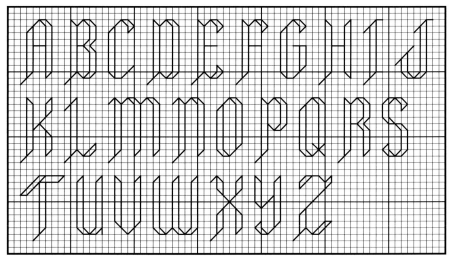

Alphabet

Tassel Illustrations

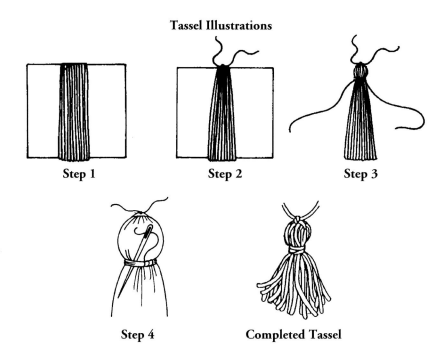

Step 1   Step 2   Step 3

Step 4   Completed Tassel

Pin-Pillow Top

DMC Pearl Cotton (Coton Perlé)
#8 white
#5 white

Fabric: 30-count white linen (**NOTE:** Cut fabric large enough to accommodate a hoop.)
Stitch count: 146H x 145W
Design size:

25-count	5⅞" x 5⅞"
27-count	5⅜" x 5⅜"
30-count	4⅞" x 4⅞"
32-count	4½" x 4½"

NOTE: Grid lines on chart and Cable-Stitch Illustration represent weave of linen.

Instructions: Work all stitches with fabric in hoop, using one strand of pearl cotton. (**NOTE:** Always remove fabric from hoop before cutting.) Use #22 tapestry needle with DMC #5 pearl cotton and #24 tapestry needle with DMC #8 pearl cotton.

Special instructions:
Area 1: Work cable stitch using DMC #8 pearl cotton, referring to Cable-Stitch-Diamond Instructions and Illustration. Backstitch initial over two threads in center of cable-stitch-diamond area, using DMC #5 pearl cotton and alphabet provided with *Bookmark.* See page 94. Work Algerian-eye-stitch variation using DMC #8 pearl cotton, referring to chart.
Area 2: Work kloster blocks using DMC #5 pearl cotton. **Very carefully** cut threads where small dots appear, cutting very close to satin-stitch bars and cutting entire group of threads at one time. Remove threads, being careful not to distort weave of fabric. Needleweave remaining threads using DMC #8 pearl cotton, inserting dove's eye in three center blocks and working a picot on outer edge of each bar. Refer to Needleweaving and Dove's-Eye Instructions and Illustration.
Area 3: Work satin stitch on left and right sides of block, using DMC #5 pearl cotton. Work hemstitch along top and bottom of block, using DMC #8 pearl

cotton and referring to Inverted Threads Rectangle Instructions—Hemstitch, and Hemstitch Illustration. **Very carefully** cut horizontal threads between rows of hemstitching, cutting close to satin-stitch borders. Remove threads, being careful not to distort weave of fabric. Work inverted-threads clusters using DMC #8 pearl cotton, referring to Inverted Threads Rectangle Instructions—Inverted Threads Clusters, and Inverted Threads Clusters Illustrations.
Area 4: Work satin stitch and hemstitch as for Area 3. **Very carefully** cut horizontal threads close to satin-stitch borders, cutting top four threads and bottom four threads and leaving four threads remaining in center between hemstitched top and bottom of area. Work four-sided stitch over remaining four threads, pulling each stitch and working from right to left.
Area 5: Work Greek cross stitch using DMC #8 pearl cotton, referring to Greek Cross Stitch Instructions and Illustrations for *Bookmark* on pages 92–93.
Area 6: Work pulled-satin-stitch variation using DMC #8 pearl cotton, referring to chart.
NOTE: Turn work and chart ninety degrees to work this area.
Area 7: Work diagonal raised-band filling using DMC #8 pearl cotton, referring to Diagonal Raised-Band Filling Instructions and Illustrations.
Area 8: Work straight stitches in direction indicated by arrows to form veins of holly leaves, using DMC #8 pearl cotton. Work raised needleweaving through the veins. Refer to Needlewoven Holly Leaves Instructions for *Bookmark* on pages 91–92.
NOTE: Cut a 36" length of pearl cotton in order to work the entire stitch with a single length.
Outer border: Count out twelve threads from edge of stitching around perimeter of design. Trim excess fabric to ⅛" beyond this point. Fold excess fabric to back. Work buttonhole stitch over four threads over folded edge, working through both thicknesses of fabric. Work a bullion knot every eighth stitch.

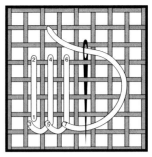

Buttonhole stitch

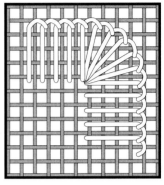

Buttonhole Stitch around a corner

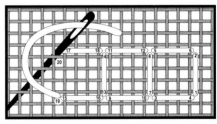

Four-Sided Stitch

Bullion Knot

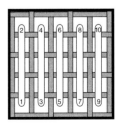

Satin Stitch

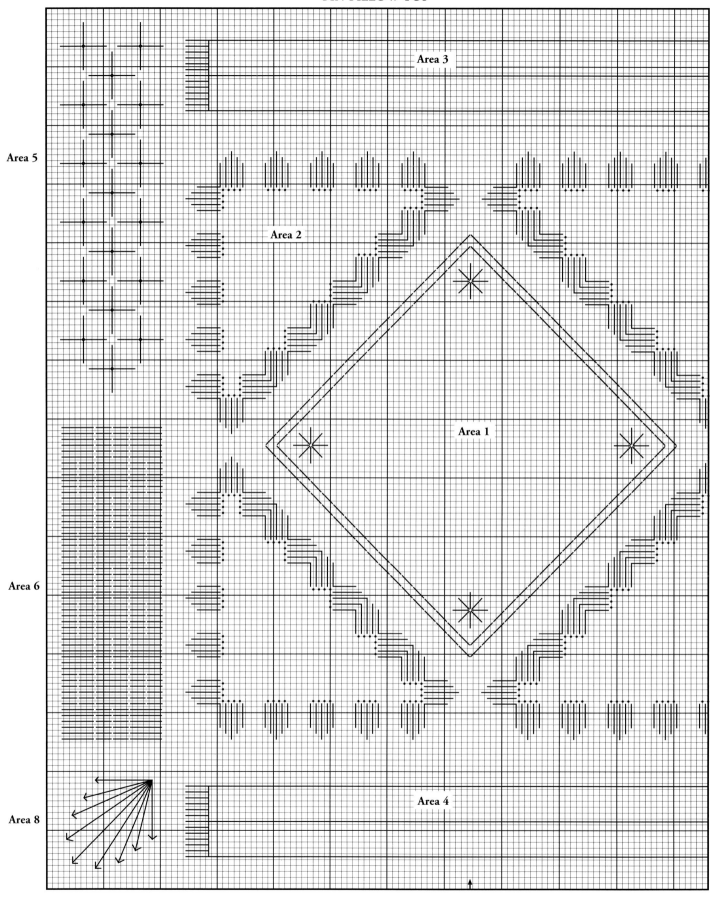

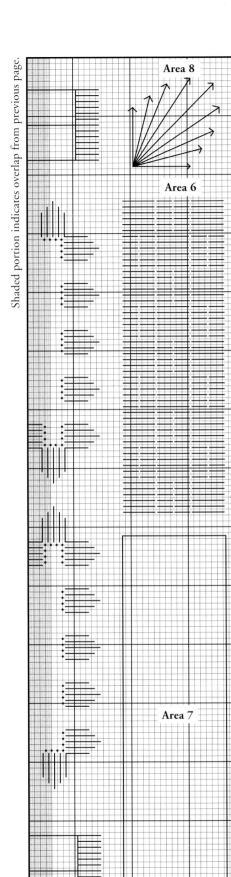

Area 8

Area 6

Area 7

Finishing instructions:
Materials:

⅜ yd. pale blue moiré fabric
1½ yds. ¼"-wide white satin ribbon
Thread to match fabric and ribbon
Wool filling
Hand-sewing needle
Paper
Pencil
Ruler
Straight pins
Scissors
Iron
Sewing machine (optional)

1. Cut two 9½" squares from blue moiré. On right side of one fabric square, center stitched piece and pin in place. Tack stitched piece to moiré from wrong side of fabric. Remove pins.

2. Place blue fabric squares together, aligning edges and placing right sides of fabric together. (**NOTE:** Be sure that grain of fabric is running in same direction on both pieces.) Pin squares together and sew around perimeter, using a ½" seam allowance and leaving a 3" opening on one side for turning. Press seams flat and turn pillow right-side out.

3. Cut a Corner Gathering Pattern from paper to use as a guide for hand-gathering each corner of pin pillow. Place pattern atop corner of pillow, aligning point of pattern with corner point of pin pillow. Lightly mark curved edge on fabric. Run a short gathering stitch along marking, pull up tightly, and knot thread to secure.

4. Stuff pillow firmly with wool filling. Hand sew opening closed.

5. Tie a small, white-ribbon bow at each corner, placing bow over gathering thread. Tack bow in place from back side, using white thread. Trim ends of ribbon on the diagonal.

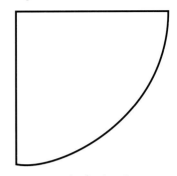

Corner Gathering Pattern

Inverted Threads Rectangle Instructions—Hemstitch

Begin hemstitch at bottom, right corner of area. Come up at 1 on Hemstitch Illustration. Count up three fabric threads and go down at this point. Cross two fabric threads to the left and come up at point 2. Count to the right two fabric threads and go down at this point. Count down three fabric threads and to the left two fabric threads and come up at point 3. Continue across in this manner to the satin stitches on the opposite side. Turn work 180 degrees and repeat to form border on opposite side.

NOTE: There should be twelve threads between the two rows of hemstitching.

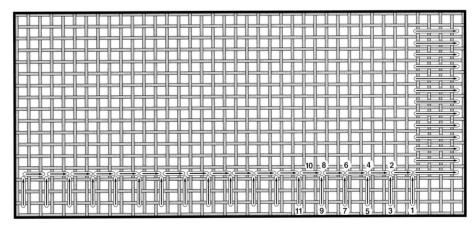

Hemstitch Illustration

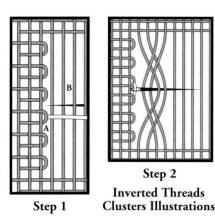

Step 1

Step 2

Inverted Threads Clusters Illustrations

Inverted Threads Rectangle Instructions—Inverted Threads Clusters

To work inverted-thread pattern, secure working thread in satin-stitch border on right side of area. Refer to Inverted Threads Clusters Illustrations, Step 1, Point A. With needle coming out in center of satin stitches on back side of work, bring needle to front between satin stitches and first remaining, vertical thread. Count over four threads and bring needle under threads three and four, having needle pointing toward starting point (Step 1, Point B). Bring tip of needle out and over first two threads. Twist the needle until it is pointing away from starting point (Step 2). Keeping needle and working thread level with fabric, pull through. Continue across. Run thread under satin stitches on back of work to secure.

Needleweaving and Dove's-Eye Instructions

Place an away waste knot at bottom of first bar, where indicated by dot on Needleweaving and Dove's-Eye Illustration. Needleweave across first half of first bar, catching waste thread as you go. Refer to Needleweaving Instructions and Illustrations for *Five-Band Sampler* on page 107 for general needleweaving technique. **NOTE:** Dotted line on Needleweaving and Dove's-Eye Illustration indicates path of waste thread.

To make picot (indicated by open thread loop on Needleweaving and Dove's-Eye Illustration) at this point, weave to side where picot will be. (**NOTE:** Work the picot on the right first.) Go down in center of bar, bringing tip of needle out on side where picot will be. The needle should be pointing toward the thread. Refer to Picot Illustration for *Five-Band Sampler* on page 108 for general picot technique. Wrap thread under needle, over needle, and under needle. Pull needle through, keeping it level with fabric. Weave to the opposite side of the bar, holding existing picot between your thumb and forefinger as you tighten the needleweaving. Make a second picot on this (opposite) side of bar. Needleweave remainder of bar. Follow numerals, in order, to move from one bar to the next, running threads under kloster blocks on back where necessary. Continue needleweaving in this manner, inserting picots as indicated on Needleweaving and Dove's-Eye Illustration, until reaching center of eighth bar.

NOTE: There is only one picot worked on the fifth, sixth, seventh, ninth, twelfth, fourteenth, fifteenth, and sixteenth bars, and no picots on the eighth and thirteenth bars.

To work a dove's eye, bring needle up on right side of eighth [thirteenth, sixteenth] bar and lay thread across to opposite bar. (**NOTE:** Numerals in brackets indicate bar numbers for placement of second and third dove's eyes, consecutively.) Holding thread in this position, put needle down in center of seventh [eighth, fifteenth] bar, swing needle over top of thread, and pull through and tighten. Lay thread straight across to opposite bar, put needle down in center of sixth [ninth, fourteenth] bar, swing needle over thread, and tighten. Lay thread straight across to opposite bar, put needle down in center of fifth [twelfth, thirteenth] bar, swing needle over thread, and tighten. Slide needle under thread coming out of center of eighth [thirteenth, sixteenth] bar. Insert needle down into center of eighth [thirteenth, sixteenth] bar and complete weaving across bar. Refer to Dove's-Eye Illustration for *Five-Band Sampler* on page 108 for general dove's-eye technique.

Continue needleweaving until reaching center of thirteenth bar. At this point, work another dove's eye following previous instructions, using first set of numerals in brackets.

Continue needleweaving until reaching center of sixteenth bar. At this point, work another dove's eye following previous instructions, using the second set of numerals in brackets.

Finish needleweaving and picots.

Repeat for each of the remaining three Hardanger triangles.

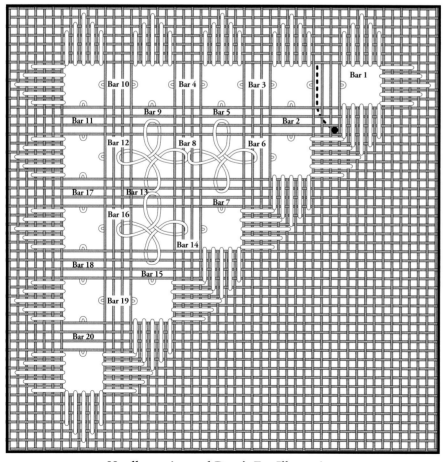

Needleweaving and Dove's Eye Illustration

Diagonal Raised-Band Filling Illustrations

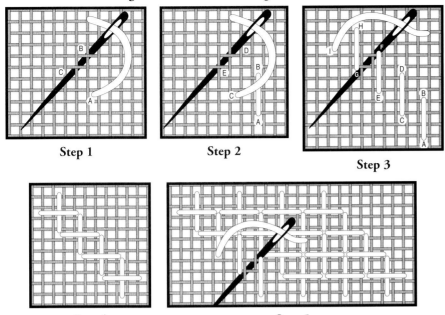

Step 1   Step 2

Step 3

Step 4   Step 5

Diagonal Raised-Band Filling Instructions

Holding work upright, begin in the top, right corner, counting down seven threads from bottom of pulled-satin-stitch variation and in two threads from edge of charted design. Bring needle up at this point and follow Diagonal Raised-Band Filling Illustrations.

Cable-Stitch-Diamond Instructions

From center of fabric, count up thirty-six threads. Begin working cable stitches, bringing needle up at 1 and going down at arrow. Cross two fabric threads to the right, bring needle up at 2, and down at arrow. Cross two fabric threads to the left, go up two fabric threads, and bring needle up at 3 and down at arrow. Refer to Cable-Stitch-Diamond Illustration. Continue in this manner, following Cable-Stitch-Diamond Illustration and referring to chart. Turn corner following stitches numbered thirty-four through thirty-eight.
(**NOTE:** Stitch thirty-four is the seventeenth stitch on the inside of the cable and stitch thirty-five is the eighteenth stitch on the outside.) At this point, turn fabric ninety degrees and repeat to form second side of diamond. Continue in this manner until all four sides are complete.

Cable-Stitch-Diamond Illustration

Five-Band Sampler

The use of ecru pearl cotton on natural linen makes a striking decorative statement in this elegant *Five-Band Sampler.* Featuring a variety of needle-working techniques, including cutwork, drawn-thread work, Hardangersøm, and needle-weaving, this eye-catching design will be perfectly at home when spotlighted in a modern setting, as shown, and will fit equally well with a grouping of samplers old or new.

Skillfully executed tone-on-tone embroidery creates unforget-table visual impact in this impressive design. A prime example of how beautiful needlework can be achieved with the use of a single thread color, this attractive Five-Band Sampler *will be a treasured addition to any needleworker's collection.*

Five-Band Sampler

DMC Pearl Cotton (Coton Perlé)
  #8   ecru
  #5   ecru

Fabric: 28-count natural Irish linen from Charles Craft, Inc.
Stitch count: 331H x 186W
Design size:

25-count	13¼" x 7½"
28-count	11⅞" x 6⅝"
32-count	10⅜" x 5⅞"
36-count	9¼" x 5¼"

NOTE: Please read instructions carefully before beginning. Grid lines on chart represent weave of linen. Use #24 tapestry needle with #8 Pearl Cotton and #22 tapestry needle with #5 Pearl Cotton. An embroidery hoop will be necessary for securing work while needleweaving. To begin each stitch, use an away waste knot unless otherwise indicated, leaving enough thread to rethread needle and secure thread under stitches.
Instructions:
Run a vertical basting line down center of fabric.
Area 1: Work kloster blocks using DMC #5 pearl cotton. **Very carefully** cut threads where small dots appear, cutting very close to the satin-stitch bars and cutting entire group of threads at one time. Remove threads, being careful not to distort weave of fabric. Needleweave remaining threads using DMC #8 pearl cotton, inserting dove's eye in center block and referring to Needleweaving Instructions. Work a picot on outer edge of each bar that borders center block.
Area 2: Work vertical satin stitch using DMC #5 pearl cotton. Work diagonal satin stitch using DMC #8 pearl cotton, stitching in direction indicated by lines on chart. Work a double knot stitch in center of each satin-stitch diamond. Work four-sided stitch between satin-stitch rows, using DMC #8 pearl cotton. Cross stitch initials and year over one thread, using DMC #8 pearl cotton and alphabet and numerals provided.
Areas 3 & 4: Work long-armed cross stitch using DMC #8 pearl cotton.
Area 5: Work two rows of long-armed cross stitch, using DMC #8 pearl cotton and having first and second rows sharing holes.
Area 6: Clip first (top) two horizontal threads in center. **Very carefully** remove the cut threads to the edges of long-armed cross stitch. Completely remove second thread. Reweave first thread into the ditch created by removing the second thread. Continue in this manner until all horizontal threads are removed or rewoven. Work inverted thread clusters using DMC #8 pearl cotton, referring to Inverted Threads Clusters Instructions.
Area 7: Clip first (top) four and last (bottom) four threads in this section in center. Remove and reweave as described in Area 6. Work diamond hemstitch using DMC #8 pearl cotton, referring to Diamond Hemstitch Instructions.
Area 8: Beginning in center of area, backstitch over two threads, using DMC #5 pearl cotton and continuing up sides of design to top. [**NOTE:** When working backstitching up sides, secure tails from inverted threads clusters (Area 6) in backstitching.] Work diagonal queen stitches using DMC #8 pearl cotton, stitching in direction indicated by arrows on chart. Work quarter, half, or full diamond eyelet stitches in larger flowers, using DMC #8 pearl cotton.
Area 9: Work ringed backstitch over three threads, using DMC #8 pearl cotton. Work drawn-thread section, referring to Drawn-Thread Special Instructions.

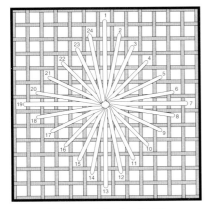

Diamond Eyelet (Full)

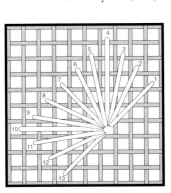

Diamond Eyelet (Diagonal Half)

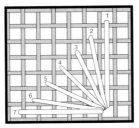

Diamond Eyelet (Quarter)

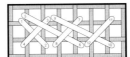

Long-Armed Cross Stitch

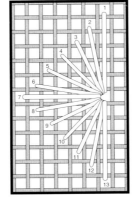

Diamond Eyelet (Half)

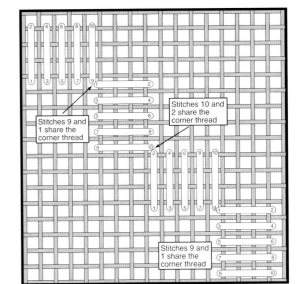

Kloster Blocks

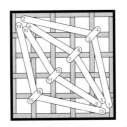

Queen Stitch (Diagonal)

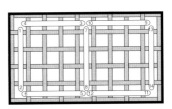

Four-Sided Stitch

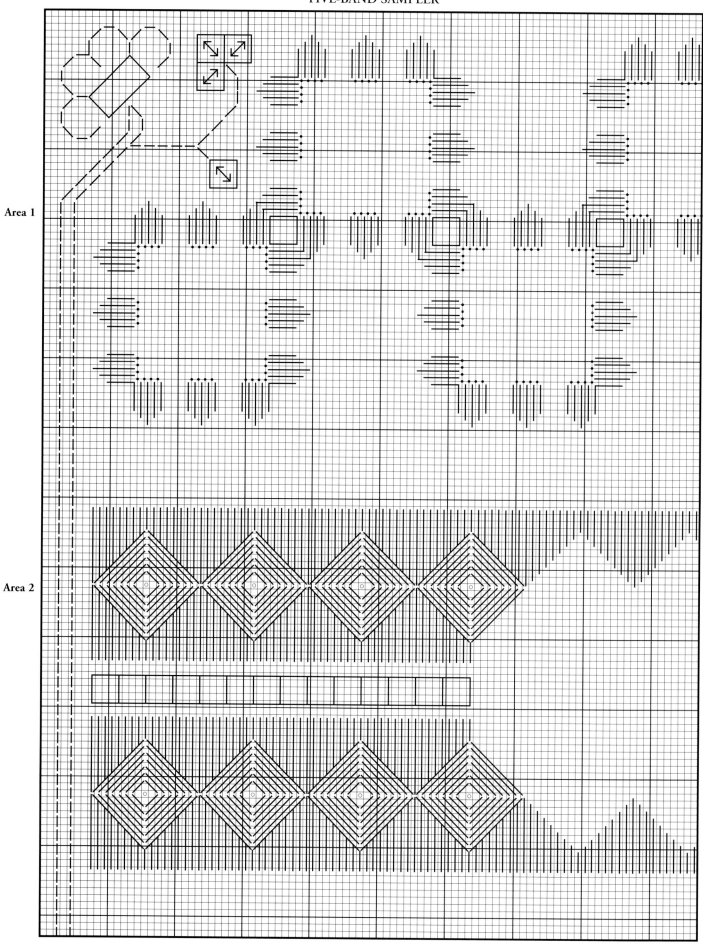

Area 1

Area 2

Shaded portion indicates overlap from previous page.

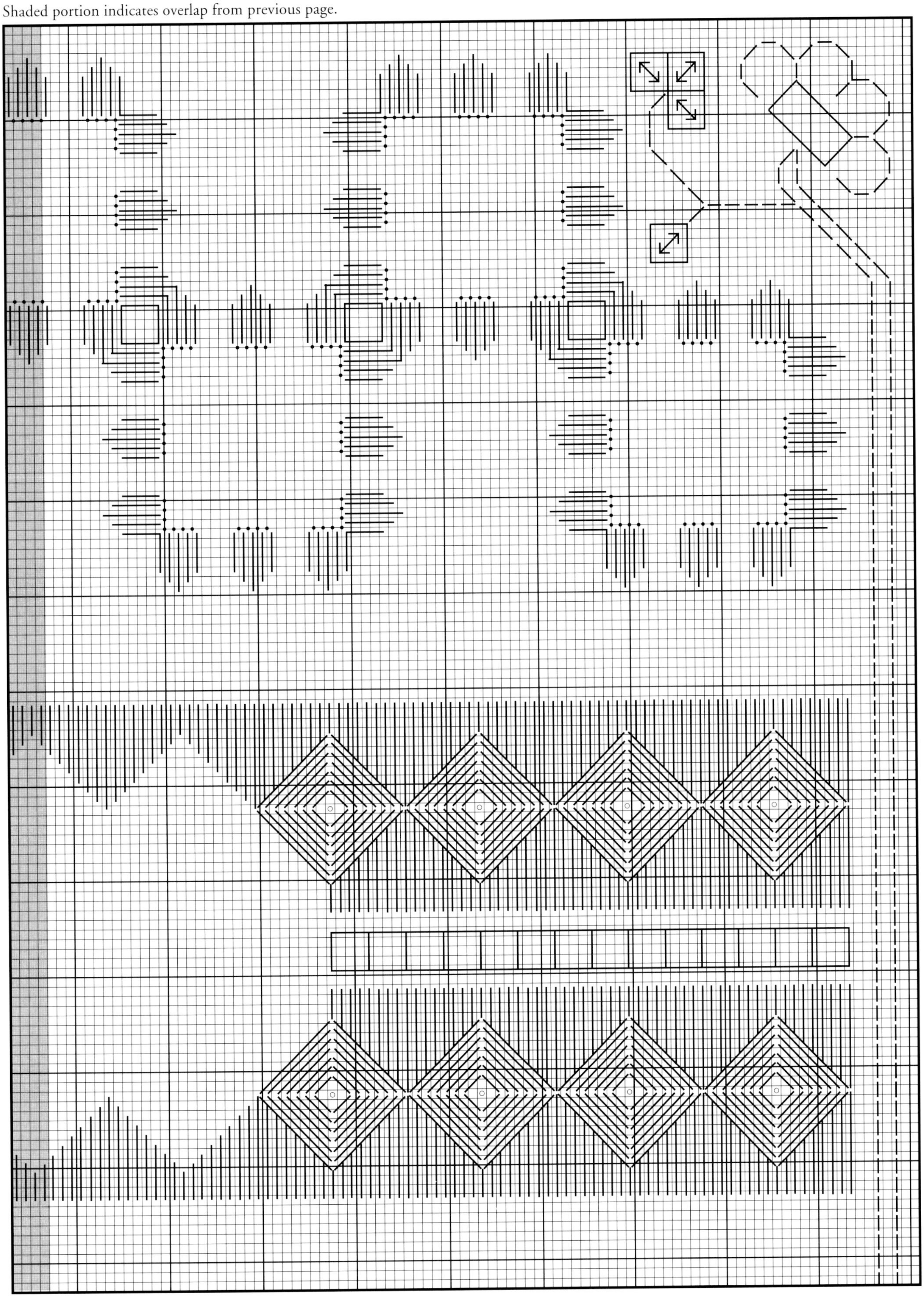

Shaded portion indicates overlap from page 102.

Area 3
Area 6
Area 5
Area 7
Area 4
Area 8

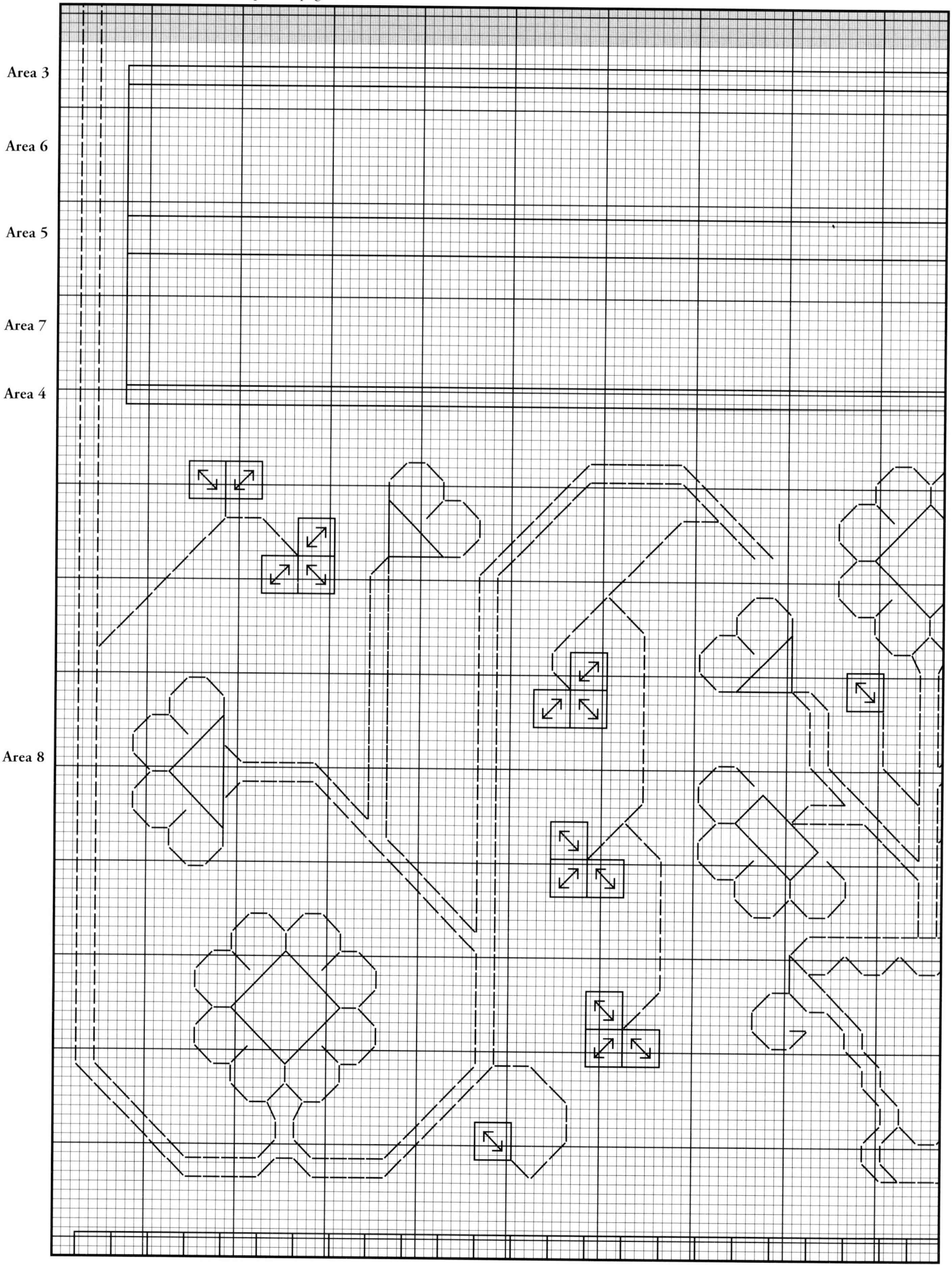

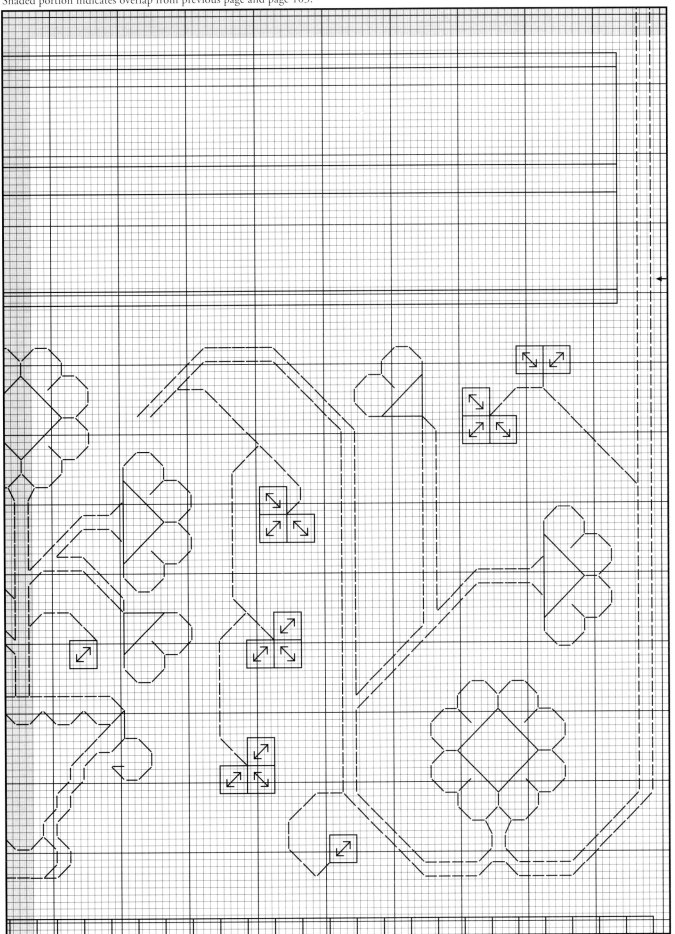

Shaded portion indicates overlap from page 104.

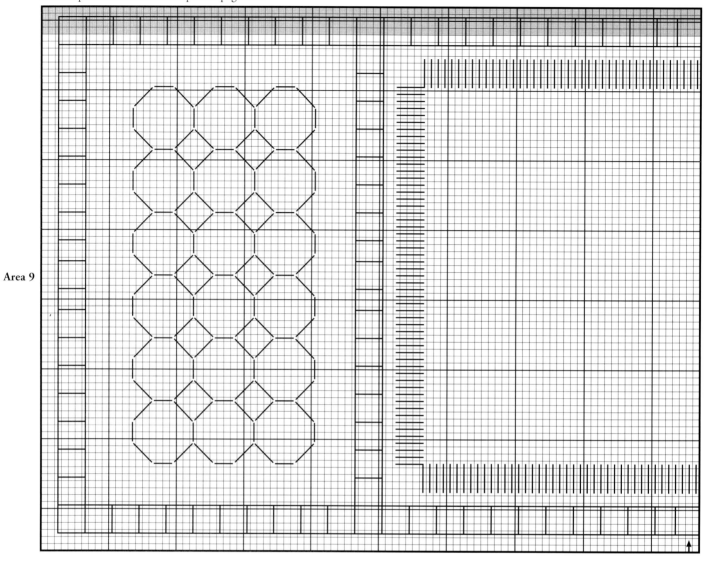

Area 9

Alphabet and Numerals

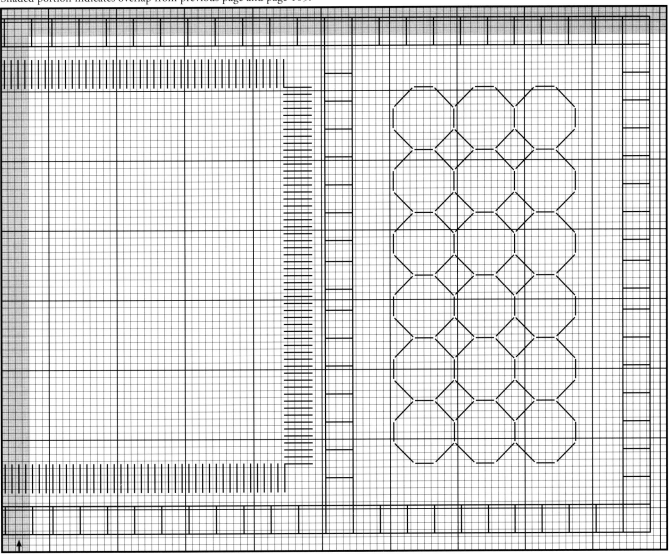

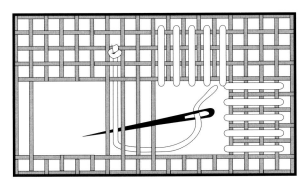

Needleweaving—Illustration 1

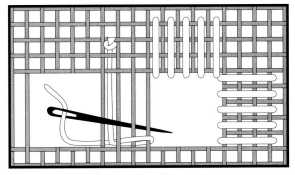

Needleweaving—Illustration 2

General Needleweaving Instructions

To begin needleweaving, use an away waste knot, placing as indicated in Needleweaving Instructions. Begin weaving over the first two fabric threads and under the last two. (Refer to Needleweaving— Illustration 1.) Continue weaving over two and under two until bar is full, using tight tension and working in a figure-eight motion (Illustration 2). Finish bar with thread toward next bar to be woven. Begin next bar by going over two fabric threads and under two fabric threads (Illustration 3).

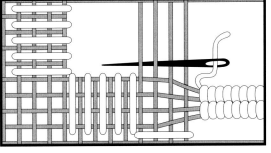

Needleweaving—Illustration 3

Needleweaving Instructions

Beginning in top, left-hand corner of kloster blocks, in center of bars one, two, four, and five, place an away waste knot where indicated by dot on Needleweaving Pattern Illustration. Needleweave across first, second, and third bars, catching waste thread while working first bar. (**NOTE:** Dotted line on Needleweaving Pattern Illustration indicates path of waste thread.) Follow numerals, in order, to move from one bar to the next, running threads under kloster blocks on back where necessary.

To make a picot (indicated by open thread loop on Needleweaving Pattern Illustration) on the top of the fourth bar, needleweave to side where picot will be. Go down in center of bar, bringing tip of needle out on side where picot will be. The needle should be pointing toward the thread. (Refer to Picot Illustration.) Wrap thread under needle, over needle, and under needle. Pull needle through, keeping it level with fabric. Weave to other side of bar, holding picot between thumb and forefinger while tightening the needleweaving. Finish weaving that bar. Continue needleweaving in this manner, inserting picots as indicated on Needleweaving Pattern Illustration, until reaching center of ninth bar. Do not work picot at this time. Instead, begin working Dove's Eye. Weave to left side of ninth bar (thread should come from back side of

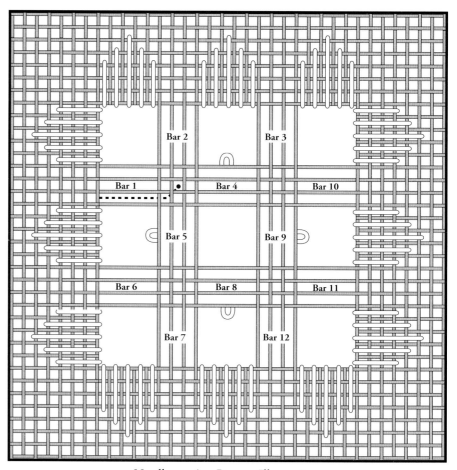

Needleweaving Pattern Illustration

bar), and lay thread across to opposite bar. Holding thread in this position, pass needle down in center of fourth bar, swing needle over top of thread, and pull through and tighten thread. Continue by laying thread

straight across to opposite bar, again holding it in this position. Pass needle down in center of fifth bar, swing needle over thread, and pull through and tighten thread. Lay thread straight across to

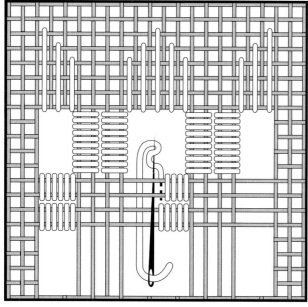

Picot Illustration

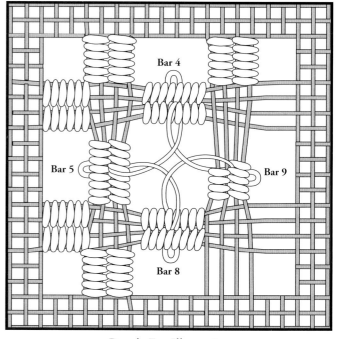

Dove's-Eye Illustration

opposite bar, again holding in position. Pass needle down in center of eighth bar, swing needle over thread, and pull through and tighten thread. Slide needle under thread coming out of center of ninth bar. Insert needle down into center of ninth bar (from front to back). Weave to opposite side of bar and work final picot. Finish needleweaving and end thread under kloster blocks.

Inverted Threads Clusters Instructions

To work inverted-thread pattern, come up in center of ditch created on left side. (Refer to Inverted Threads Clusters Illustrations, Step 1, Point A.) Count over eight threads and bring needle under threads eight, seven, six, and five, having needle pointing toward starting point (Step 1, Point B). Bring tip of needle out and over first four threads. Twist needle until it is pointing away from starting point (Step 2). Keeping needle and working thread level with fabric, pull through. Continue across, leaving a tail to be worked into back-stitching later.

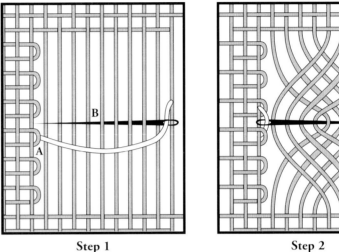

Step 1 **Step 2**
Inverted Threads Clusters Illustrations

Diamond Hemstitch Instructions

Work from right to left, pulling gently on right side of fabric. Bring needle up at numerals and down at arrows. Work all the way across, following numerals. End thread. Begin a new thread and work all the way across, following letters.

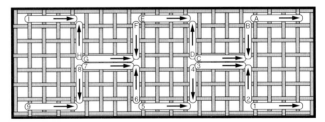

Diamond Hemstitch Illustration

Ringed Backstitch Instructions

Beginning on left side of design and working from left to right, bring needle up at numerals and down at arrows, pulling gently when coming from back to front. (**NOTE:** There are three ringed backstitches in each of the six, horizontal rows. The left side of the second stitch is the right side of the previous stitch, and will have two strands of thread sharing the same holes. The same applies to the top and bottom of the stitches in row one and row two, row two and row three, etc.) Repeat on right side of design.

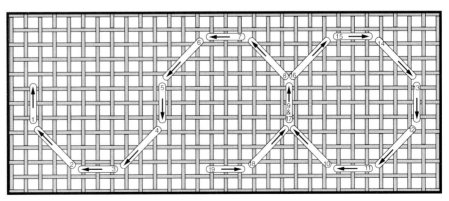

Ringed Backstitch Illustration

Drawn-Thread Special Instructions

On back of fabric, beginning sixteen threads below bottom of Area 8 and on center, vertical line, count to the left thirty-nine threads and begin a horizontal basting line, going over two threads, then under two threads, etc., covering seventy-eight threads. Twenty basting stitches will be showing. Secure thread out of the way of stitching. Using another basting thread, begin in the same hole as the one in which the previous stitch ended, and run a vertical basting thread covering fifty-four threads. Fourteen basting threads will be showing. Secure thread out of the way of stitching. Continue basting in this manner to form a rectangle containing seventy-eight vertical threads and fifty-four horizontal threads.

NOTE: Each of the four corners should have basting threads over two on the top, going both directions, with the corners sharing holes.

Just inside top, horizontal basting line and just left of vertical, center basting line, locate first two horizontal threads. (**NOTE:** There should be vertical basting threads running over these threads on left and right sides of rectangle.) Carefully clip these two fabric threads. Skip two horizontal fabric threads. Clip the next two horizontal fabric threads. Again, there should be vertical basting threads running over these threads on left and right sides of rectangle. Continue in this manner to bottom of rectangle.

Count down seven basting stitches on left basting line to find horizontal center of rectangle. Clip vertical fabric threads along horizontal center, using same method as for clipping horizontal threads.

Carefully place hoop on fabric and, on back of fabric, begin unweaving cut fabric threads from the center to the outer basting threads. Use basting stitches to secure fabric threads.

NOTE: At this point, there should be a grid consisting of nineteen horizontal bars and thirteen vertical bars.

Turn to front of fabric. Thread needle with length of DMC #8 pearl cotton, cut long enough to work all the way down one bar. Bring needle up in "hole" in top, left corner, and begin wrapping vertical bar, wrapping twice between horizontal bars, and pulling gently. (Refer to Wrapping-Bars Illustrations.) (**NOTE:** Be sure to catch tail of thread under wrapping.) End working thread the same as beginning, make a tacking stitch, and run tail under wrappings of bar. Continue in this manner until all vertical and horizontal bars are completely wrapped. Remove all basting threads.

Work satin stitch around grid, using DMC #5 pearl cotton. Bring needle up four threads outside the grid, and go down in the grid, catching previously cut fabric threads underneath stitches. Work satin stitch around perimeter of grid.

Work four-sided stitch around drawn-thread area, using DMC #8 pearl cotton and catching previously cut fabric threads under stitches.

NOTE: There are compensation stitches in four-sided area. The stitches in the center of the grid are worked over three vertical threads and four horizontal threads.

Needleweave the grid using DMC #5 pearl cotton. Weaving the grid is accomplished by going over one bar, under the next, over the next, etc. (Refer to Needleweaving Design Illustration.) (**NOTE:** Broken lines show path of thread on back of work.) Each square on Weaving Design chart represents one hole in grid. When covering three squares of chart, weaving covers four bars of grid. For each section, weave in direction indicated by symbols on Weaving Design chart.

In center of grid, where there are four "holes," work whipped stitch around center, bringing needle up through hole at A. (Refer to Whipped-Stitch Illustration.) Repeat pattern until bars are full, turning fabric as you stitch.

Finish four-sided-stitch border around ringed backstitch on both sides, using DMC #8 pearl cotton.

NOTE: As before, there are compensation stitches.

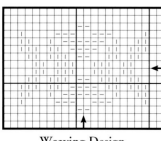

Weaving Design

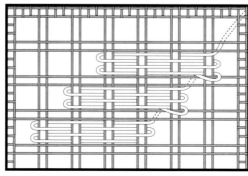

Needleweaving Design Illustration

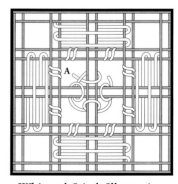

Whipped-Stitch Illustration

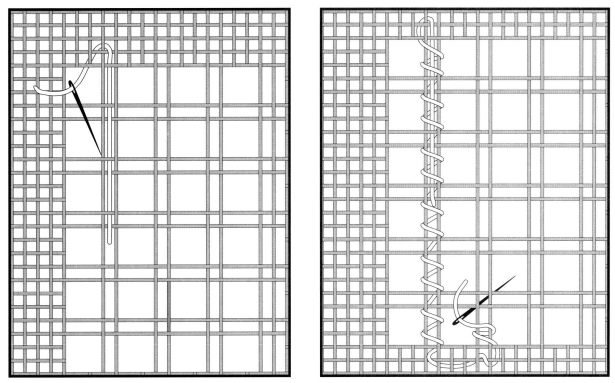

Wrapping-Bars Illustrations

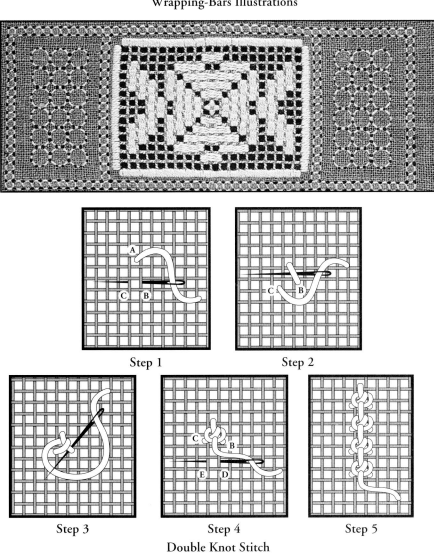

Step 1

Step 2

Step 3

Step 4

Step 5

Double Knot Stitch

Rose-Wreath Chatelaine

Detailed stitchery, complementary silk ribbon, and clever finishing techniques are combined to create this endearing *Rose-Wreath Chatelaine.* Including a needlebook, a pin keep, and a scissor sheath, this attractive ensemble will allow the needleart enthusiast to carry the tools for her hobby in unequalled style. Attention to detail makes this imaginative creation a standout. In addition to the attractive stitchery used for each piece, this chatelaine features a variety of utilitarian qualities. The pages of the needlebook include labeling that will allow the needleworker to store her needles properly and be able to locate the size needle she needs at a glance. The scissors are attached to the chatelaine with their own ribbon, thus preventing them from being lost when they are in use outside the sheath. An alphabet and numerals chart can be used by the stitcher to embellish the backs of the holders with the desired initials and, excluding the scissor sheath, the year in which the project was completed. Inspired by chatelaines from the past, this design features a ring-and-ribbon

"head" that is reminiscent of styles seen during the early years of the twentieth century. To learn more about chatelaines, turn to *Chatelaines: Traveling Companions of an Intimate Persuasion,* on page 54.

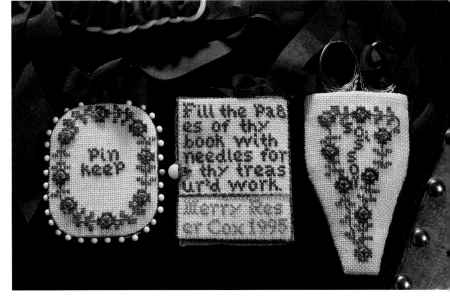

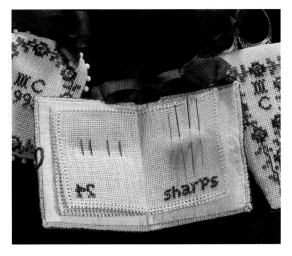

ROSE-WREATH CHATELAINE

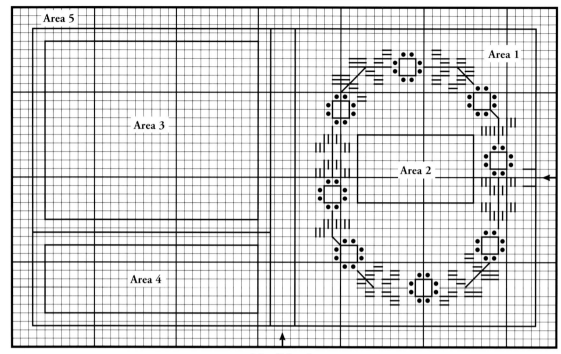

Needlebook

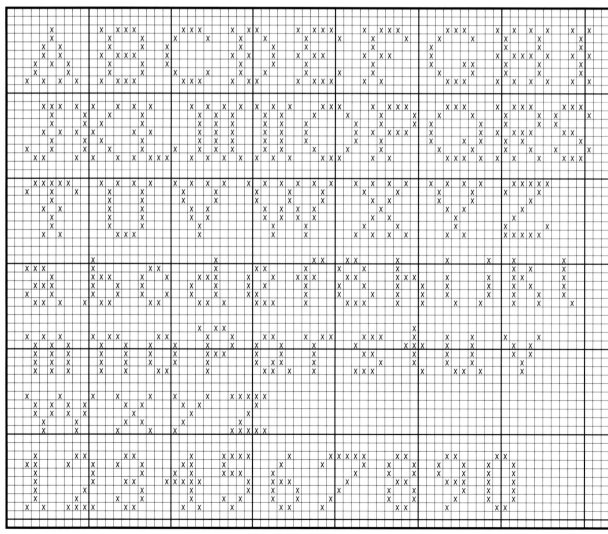

Alphabet and Numerals

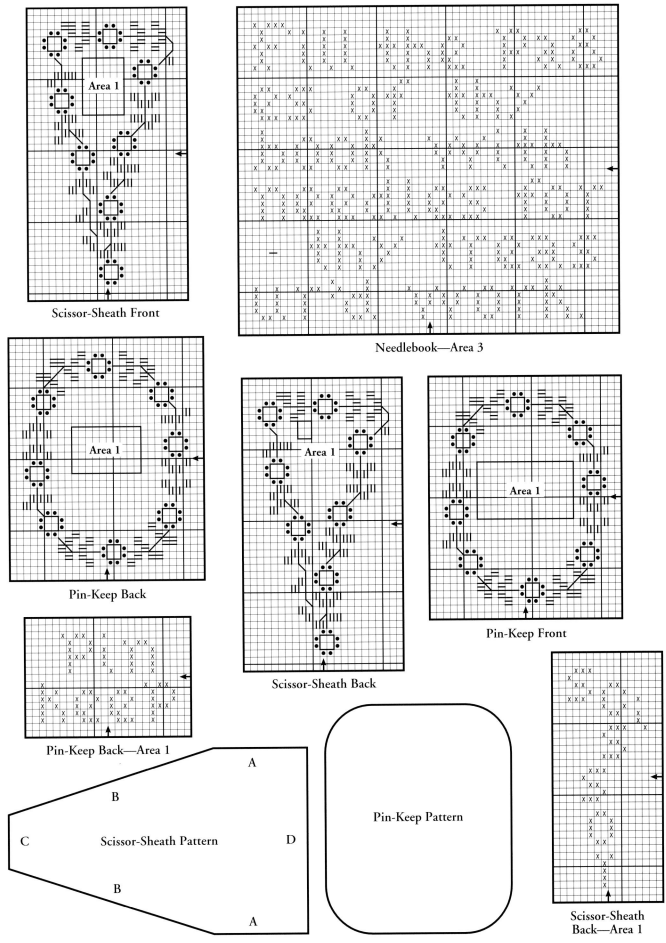

Scissor-Sheath Front

Needlebook—Area 3

Pin-Keep Back

Area 1

Area 1

Scissor-Sheath Back

Pin-Keep Front

Pin-Keep Back—Area 1

Scissor-Sheath Pattern

Pin-Keep Pattern

Scissor-Sheath
Back—Area 1

Rose-Wreath Chatelaine

	DMC	Kreinik		
	DMC	FT	Soie d'Alger	
X	221	2221	4624	pink, dk.
bs	936	2937	2136	avocado, vy. dk.
ss	3052	—	3714	green-gray, med.

The Caron Collection Wildflowers
- 056 Potpourri

DMC #80 Tatting Cotton
ecru

Fabric: 26-count golden flax linen from Wichelt Imports, Inc.
Needlebook
(**NOTE:** Cut one 7" x 5" piece for *Needlebook* and two 4" x 5½" pieces for *Needlebook* pages.)
Pin Keep
(**NOTE:** Cut two 5" squares.)
Scissor Sheath
(**NOTE:** Cut two 5" x 7" pieces.)
Design size:
Needlebook
26-count   2⅝" x 4¼"
Pin Keep
26-count   2½" x 2"
Scissor Sheath
26-count   3¼" x 2"

NOTE: Please read instructions carefully before beginning. When working with Caron Wildflowers, complete one stitch at a time.

Instructions: Cross stitch over two threads, using one strand of Wildflowers unless otherwise indicated. Backstitch (bs) using two strands 936/2937/2136. Work satin stitch using two strands 936/2937/2136, working in direction indicated by lines on chart. Work cable stitch using one strand of Wildflowers.

Special instructions:
Needlebook:
Area 1: Work Smyrna cross stitch over four threads in center of flowers, using one strand of Wildflowers. Work straight stitch (ss) in each corner of Smyrna cross, using two strands 3052/—/3714.
Area 2: Cross stitch initials and year over one thread, using one strand 221/2221/4624 and alphabet and numerals provided, and leaving two threads between initials and year.

Area 3: Cross stitch over one thread, using one strand of floss.
Area 4: Cross stitch name and year over one thread, using one strand 3052/—/3714 and alphabet and numerals provided.
Area 5: Work cable stitch around outside border, spine, and between verse and name blocks on back of *Needlebook,* where heavy line appears, using one strand of Wildflowers.
NOTE: When working cable stitch, work from left to right. When corner is reached, go to back of work and go under previous stitch to anchor; then come back up in same corner hole, turn work, and continue as indicated. To form button loop, work cable stitch to point indicated on right side of *Needlebook.* Bring needle up at A, then down at B, leaving a loop of thread. Repeat. Bring needle up at A and work Hedebo buttonhole stitch on loops until loops are completely covered. Bring needle down at B and continue cable stitch.
Pin-Keep **Front:**
Work floral section as for *Needlebook.*
Area 1: Cross stitch initials and year over one thread, using one strand 221/2221/4624 and alphabet and numerals provided.
Pin-Keep **Back:**
Work floral section as for *Needlebook.*
Area 1: Cross stitch over one thread, using one strand of floss.
Scissor-Sheath **Front:**
Work floral section as for *Needlebook.*
Area 1: Cross stitch initials over one thread, using one strand 221/2221/4624 and alphabet provided, and leaving two threads between initials.
Scissor-Sheath **Back:**
Work floral section as for *Needlebook.*
Area 1: Cross stitch over one thread, using one strand of floss.
NOTE: Box on chart indicates placement of first *S* in *scissor.*

Finishing instructions:
Note: For these projects, a general list of materials has been given. Specific materials for each project have been listed separately.

General materials:
#24 tapestry needle
Hand-sewing needle
Sewing thread to match linen and ribbon
Embroidery scissors
Paper-cutting scissors
Iron and press cloth

Needlebook
Materials:
7" x 5" piece ivory silk (for lining)
Two 7" x 5" pieces medium-weight iron-on interfacing
¼" button with shank

1. Complete stitching following instructions given.
2. Press face-down atop soft cloth.
3. Trim seam allowances to ⅝" from exterior cable-stitch border.
4. Cut one piece of interfacing and one piece of lining to fit inside cable-stitch border area. Cut another piece of interfacing slightly smaller.
5. Bond larger piece of interfacing to wrong side of needlework, inside cable-stitch border area. Fold seam allowances along cable-stitch outline as follows. Fold and miter corners; then fold in sides. Baste corners in place.
NOTE: Cable stitch will be edge of needlebook.
6. Sew on button where indicated by — on chart for Area 3.
7. Bond smaller piece of interfacing to wrong side of lining fabric. Trim seam allowances to ½". Fold seam allowances as in Step 5. Blind stitch lining to wrong side of *Needlebook,* leaving a ½" opening at top for inserting ribbon when attaching to chatelaine.
8. Finish edges of two 4" x 5½" pieces of linen with Nun's stitch, using one strand DMC #80 Tatting Cotton. Begin Nun's stitch 1" from top and left sides of linen. Trim excess linen. (**NOTE:** Finished pages will measure 2" x 3½".) Press pages. Place the linen pages atop *Needlebook,* stacking one page atop the other, folding in center, and aligning center fold with spine. Whipstitch in place along spine.
NOTE: Needle sizes can be stitched onto lower-right side of pages by cross stitching over one thread, using one strand 221/2221/4624.

Pin Keep
Materials:
4" x 6" piece posterboard
4" x 6" piece fusible fleece
½ yd. 2mm-wide burgundy silk ribbon
Thirty 1⅜" glass-head pins

1. Complete stitching following instructions given.
2. Press each side face-down atop soft cloth.

3. Sew two rows of gathering stitches; the first row ½" beyond needlework area, and the second row ¼" beyond first row. Trim linen ½" beyond second gathering-stitch row.

4. Trace Pin-Keep Pattern onto posterboard. Cut two. Bond fusible fleece to each piece of posterboard.

NOTE: Fleece-covered side of posterboard will be on inside of *Pin Keep*.

5. Gather *Pin-Keep* front around posterboard and lace securely. Repeat for *Pin-Keep* back. Blind stitch front to back, leaving ½" opening at top for inserting ribbon when attaching to chatelaine.

6. Tack 2mm-wide silk ribbon over blind stitching, inserting ends into opening at top.

Scissor Sheath
Materials:
2 recipe cards
Two 5" x 7" pieces fusible fleece
Two 5" x 7" pieces medium-weight iron-on interfacing
Two 5" x 7" pieces ivory silk (for lining)
½ yd. 2mm-wide burgundy silk ribbon

1. Complete stitching following instructions given.

2. Press each side face-down atop soft cloth.

3. Trace Scissor-Sheath Pattern onto recipe cards, lining fabric, and fusible fleece. Cut two of each. Bond fusible fleece to recipe cards.

4. Fold *Scissor-Sheath* front around recipe card, placing fleece side next to wrong side of needlework and centering stitched design. Trim seam allowances to ¾" from fold. Fold top sides (A) first and lace securely, then bottom sides (B), bottom (C), and top (D). Repeat for *Scissor-Sheath* back.

5. Trace Scissor-Sheath Pattern onto interfacing, and cut two slightly smaller than pattern. Bond each to wrong side of lining fabric. Trim seam allowance to ½".

6. Blind stitch one lining piece to *Scissor-Sheath* front. Repeat for *Scissor-Sheath* back. Blind stitch front to back along sides and bottom. Tack 2mm-wide silk ribbon over blind stitching, placing ends over top and inside sheath on each side.

Chatelaine
Materials:
5 yds. 13mm-wide burgundy silk ribbon
1 yd. 35mm-wide burgundy silk ribbon
Ten ⅝" plastic rings

Embroidery scissors (**NOTE:** This pair can be the same as was listed in general materials and used to make this project.)

1. Cut three 10" lengths from 13mm-wide silk ribbon. Set aside. Measure 17" of remaining 13mm-wide silk ribbon. Fold ribbon back on itself until there are eight layers. **Do not** cut. The two loose ends will be at the top. Place a straight pin through layers at top and bottom for better control.

2. Weave ribbons through nine rings, leaving 4" at top. Remove straight pins.

3. Place ribbons through separate ring at top and loop around and up through inside of first ring in the woven section. All loose ends are now inside this loop. Tack ribbons in center, under single ring. Make large bow using 35mm-wide silk ribbon. Tack bow where ribbons were tacked together.

4. Lay piece flat with loops of ribbon stacked one atop the other. The top ribbon is #1. Attach needlework pieces and embroidery scissors to the four loops of ribbon as follows. Attach embroidery scissors to loop of ribbon #3 by placing loop through one finger hole of scissors and looping back over. Tack *Pin Keep* to loop of ribbon #1, inserting ribbon into small opening at top until *Pin Keep* is even with scissors. Tack *Needlebook* to loop of ribbon #2, and *Scissor Sheath* to loop of ribbon #4 in the same manner. Make three bows using the 10" lengths of 13mm-wide silk ribbon. Tack a bow where chatelaine ribbon is attached to each holder.

5. Insert glass-head pins around edges of *Pin Keep*, spacing evenly for a decorative effect.

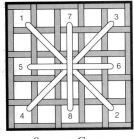
Smyrna Cross

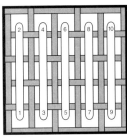
Satin Stitch (Vertical)

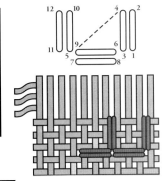
Nun's Stitch

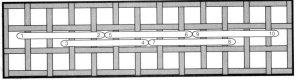
Cable Stitch

Ring Weaving Illustration

Hedebo Buttonhole Stitch

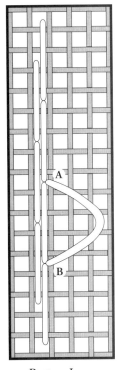
Button Loop Illustration

The Promise & Twisted-Ribbon Samplers

An assortment of unusual dividing bands, simple messages of faith, the stitcher's initials, and the years in which the stitchery was completed comprise these charming pieces. This duet of diminutive samplers features a variety of stitches worked in floss colors that will complement most any decorating theme. Including cross, satin, Algerian eye, queen, double running, Bosnia, and long-armed cross stitches, these tiny treasures will pique the interest of the needleworker who enjoys learning the techniques to work added stitches. These miniatures will be pleasing, both while they are being stitched and when they are put to decorative use in the sampler enthusiast's home.

THE PROMISE SAMPLER

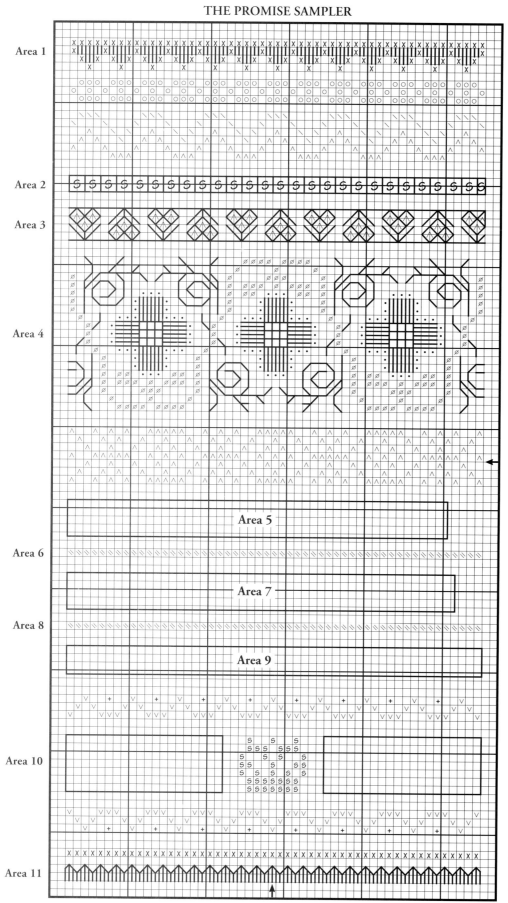

Area 1
Area 2
Area 3
Area 4
Area 5
Area 6
Area 7
Area 8
Area 9
Area 10
Area 11

The Promise Sampler

Kreinik
DMC Soie

DMC	FT	d'Alger	
∧ 316	2316	4634	mauve, med.
S 732	2732	2214	olive
╲ 733	2734	2212	olive, med.
• 739	2738	4241	tan, ul. lt.
╲ 778	2778	4631	mauve, lt.
● 839	2839	3436	beige-brown, dk.
X 924	2924	206	gray-green, vy. dk.
v 926	2926	1745	gray-green, dk.
+ 928	2928	1742	gray-green, lt.
⌀ 3052	—	3714	green-gray, med.
○ 3053	—	3713	green-gray
712	ecru	creme	cream
3051	—	3715	green-gray, dk.

Fabric: 35-count antique white linen
Stitch count: 104H x 53W
Design size:

25-count	8⅜" x 4¼"
28-count	7⅜" x 3¾"
30-count	6⅞" x 3½"
35-count	6" x 3"

Instructions: Cross stitch over two threads, using two strands of floss unless otherwise indicated. **NOTE:** Backstitch may be substituted for double running stitch.

Special instructions:

Area 1: Work satin stitch in center of each triangle, using two strands 928/2928/1742.

Area 2: Work Algerian eye stitch using two strands of floss.

Area 3: Work double running stitch for vine and leaves, using one strand 3051/—/3715. Work queen stitch for flowers, using one strand of floss.

Area 4: Work double running stitch for tendrils, using one strand 3051/—/3715. Work satin stitch for flower petals, using two strands 712/ecru/creme and stitching in direction indicated by lines on chart. Work double running stitch for center of each flower, using one strand 839/2839/3436.

Areas 5, 7, & 9: Cross stitch over one thread, using one strand of floss.

Area 6: Work Bosnia stitch using two strands of floss.

Area 8: Work long-armed cross stitch using two strands of floss.

Area 10: Cross stitch initials and year using alphabet and numerals provided.

Area 11: Work satin stitch using two strands 924/2924/206.

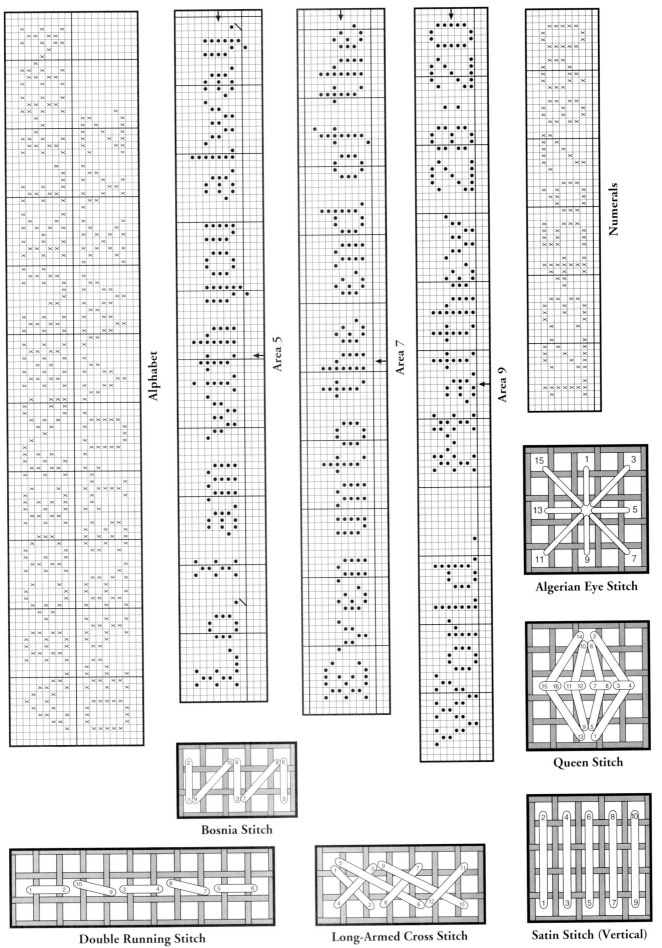

Alphabet

Area 5

Area 7

Area 9

Numerals

Algerian Eye Stitch

Queen Stitch

Bosnia Stitch

Satin Stitch (Vertical)

Double Running Stitch

Long-Armed Cross Stitch

123

Twisted-Ribbon Sampler

DMC	Kreinik FT	DMC Soie d'Alger		
○ 315	2315	4646	mauve, dk.	
• 316	2316	4634	mauve, med.	
★ 355	2303	2636	terra cotta, dk.	
● 780	2782	2521	topaz, vy. dk.	
C 797	2797	4924	royal blue	
／ 799	2799	1434	delft, med.	
X 935	—	2126	avocado, dk.	
∧ 3779	2759	2912	terra cotta, ul. vy. lt.	
356	2356	4612	terra cotta, med.	
367	2320	1835	pistachio, dk.	
470	2469	2125	avocado, lt.	
3740	—	4635	antique violet, dk.	
3777	2354	2636	terra cotta, vy. dk.	
3778	2356	2914	terra cotta, lt.	
838	2938	4136	beige-brown, vy. dk.	

Fabric: 35-count antique white linen
Stitch count: 100H x 50W
Design size:

25-count	8" x 4"
28-count	7⅛" x 3½"
30-count	6⅝" x 3⅜"
35-count	5¾" x 2⅞"

Instructions: Cross stitch over two threads, using two strands of floss unless otherwise indicated. **NOTE:** Backstitch may be substituted for double running stitch.

Special instructions:

Area 1: Work double running stitch using one strand 3740/—/4635.

Area 2: Work double running stitch for vine, using one strand 470/2469/2125. Work Algerian eye stitch for flowers, using two strands of floss.

Area 3: Work satin stitch using two strands 355/2303/2636.

Area 4: Work vertical satin stitch using two strands 356/2356/4612. Work horizontal satin stitch using two strands 3777/2354/2636.

Area 5: Work double running stitch for flower petals, using one strand 3778/2356/2914. Work double running stitch for tendrils, using one strand 367/2320/1835. Backstitch around center of flowers, using one strand 838/2938/4136.

Areas 6 & 7: Work double running stitch using one strand 367/2320/1835.

Area 8: Cross stitch initials and year using alphabet and numerals provided.

Area 9: Work double running stitch using one strand 315/2315/4646.

Area 1   Area 2   Area 3   Area 4   Area 5

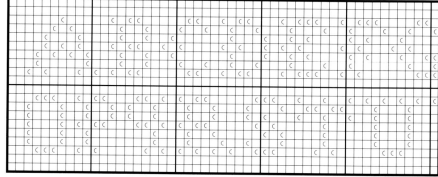

Area 10: Work satin stitch using two strands 315/2315/4646 for top portion of band, and two strands 3740/—/4635 for bottom portion of band.

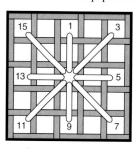

Algerian Eye Stitch

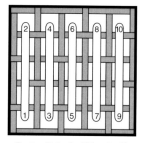

Satin Stitch (Vertical)

Shaded portion indicates overlap from previous page.

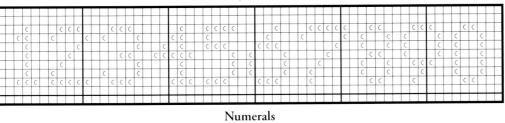

Area 6

Area 7

Area 8

Area 9

Area 10

Shaded portion indicates overlap from previous page.

Alphabet

Numerals

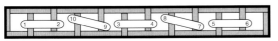

Double Running Stitch

Victorian Treasures

While many needlewomen of modern times tend to take basic supplies for plying their craft for granted, stitchers of generations past were far more cautious with their materials. Most households, even those of respectable financial means, had limited resources with which to acquire the tools of the trade for the lady of the house. What by today's standards constitutes a modest supply may very well have been viewed as abundance, or even excess, by the standards applicable during times past. Because of her limited resources, the needleworker's tools became objects of great value, which were protected with vigor from loss or damage. Perhaps then, it was inevitable that holders—for everything from needles to scissors—were an essential and valued part of the needlewoman's possessions. And during a time when few women were granted the privilege of money, these diminutive protectors were fashioned from every scrap imaginable; some were even embellished with human hair, and were given as gifts of friendship from one woman to another. Inspired by sewing accessories from days gone by, this charming *Victorian Treasures* trio—including a fan-shaped needlecase, a boot-shaped scissors sheath, and a pincushion that

was fashioned after the canoe-shaped, antique piece shown with it—was constructed using millinery felt from vintage hats, and kid leather from the type of gloves that many of us wore, as children, with our Sunday best. Completed with embroidery stitches and silk-ribbon bows, this threesome will allow the avid stitcher to keep her favorite needleworking supplies close at hand while providing attractive repositories for them.

Victorian Treasures

NOTE: For these projects, a general list of materials and instructions have been given. Specific materials and instructions for each project have been listed separately.

General materials:
Vintage felt hat(s) in color(s) of your choice
Mercerized thread to match felt
Polyester filling
Hand-sewing needle
Straight pins
Marking pencil
Scissors
Iron
Small needle-nose pliers (optional)

NOTE: The designer recommends using millinery felt to obtain the best results. The body of this type of felt is much heavier than that of the readily available felt in current manufacture, and will stand up to the embellishing stitches and shaping required to complete these pieces. In addition to attics, antique stores, and estate auctions, the would-be hat seeker should also remember vintage clothing stores as a possible source for old felt hats.

General instructions:
Preparing the felt
Remove all ornamentation, including wire, hat band, etc., from hat. Cut hat in half. Launder felt by machine, using warm water and laundry detergent. While felt is still damp, press with a hot iron until reasonably flat. Hang to air dry.

Making silk-ribbon rosettes
To make silk-ribbon rosettes, thread hand-sewing needle with sewing thread and place a knot in thread end. Beginning at one end of the length of silk ribbon, catch ribbon through the center, with needle, at regular intervals, starting with ¼" loops and graduating to 1" loops for the center of the rosettes. Graduate back down to smaller loops, holding all loops on the needle as you work. When rosette is desired size, hold between fingers and pull thread through. Run needle and thread back through center and knot to anchor. Trim ribbon ends.
NOTE: If using two colors of ribbon, place one atop the other and treat as one.

Victorian Fan Needlecase
Materials:
9" square small-print fabric to match felt hat (for lining)
9" square coordinating flannel **or** chamois cloth (for needle pages)
¾ yd. **each** ⅛"-wide silk ribbon in two complementary colors (for ribbon rosette) (**NOTE:** Designer used dark mauve and medium pink.)
1 yd. ⅜"-wide edging lace
2¾" x 1½" piece coordinating solid fabric (for sentiment pocket)
Embroidery floss (**NOTE:** Designer used medium green, light green, medium pink, light pink, pale yellow, tan, and light blue.)
Crewel-embroidery needle
Fine-line permanent-ink marking pen
Pinking shears

1. Pin fan pattern right-side up atop felt. Trace around pattern. Remove pattern and repeat. Remove pattern and cut out felt shapes. Set aside.
2. Pin needle-page pattern right-side up atop flannel or chamois cloth. Trace around pattern. Remove pattern and repeat for second needle page. Cut out needle pages, using pinking shears for curved edge. Set aside.
3. Pin lining pattern atop small-print fabric. Trace around pattern. Remove pattern and repeat for second lining piece. Cut out lining pieces, using pinking shears for the two straight sides and leaving a ¼" seam allowance along curved edge.
4. Fold seam allowance of lining pieces under, baste, and press. Set aside.
5. Work embroidery on one fan piece, referring to pattern on page 131 for color placement. This will be front of fan. Work French knots for center of each rose and under leaves, using six strands of floss. Work bullion knots for roses and leaves, using six strands of floss. Work chain stitch for ribs of fan, using six strands of floss. Work semicircle above neck of fan in a double row of lazy-daisy chain, using six strands of floss. Work buttonhole stitch along scalloped edge of fan, using two strands of floss.
NOTE: Needle-nose pliers may be helpful for pulling needle and threads through felt.
6. Turn edges of sentiment pocket under ¼" toward wrong side of fabric, baste, and press.
7. Write, print, or embroider desired sentiment on right side of sentiment pocket, using fine-line permanent-ink marking pen or embroidery floss and needle. Refer to back schematic for placement. Work embroidery on pocket. Work French knots for flowers, using two strands of floss. Work lazy-daisy stitches for leaves, using two strands of floss.
8. Whipstitch sentiment pocket to back of remaining fan piece.
9. Attach lace edging to fan front and back along scalloped edges, attaching to inside (unembellished side) of each piece, using small running stitches, and pinching in fullness as you sew.
10. Whipstitch lining pieces to inside front and back of fan, being careful not to pierce through to right side of felt.
11. Attach needle pages to inside of fan back along straight edges, using small running stitches.
12. Weave two 8" lengths of ribbon under bullion-knot stems on front of fan.
13. Holding front and back pieces of fan together with right sides out, work buttonhole stitch around ⅔ of neck of fan, using two strands of floss. Stuff neck firmly with polyester filling. Work buttonhole stitch around remainder of neck of fan.
14. Work buttonhole stitch along the two outer edges of fan, using two strands of floss and catching ends of woven ribbon in seams.
15. Tack silk-ribbon rosette to fan at neck.

Victorian Boot Scissors Sheath
Materials:
Vintage kid glove
6" square small-print fabric to match felt hat (for lining)
Embroidery floss (**NOTE:** Designer used medium green and pale yellow.)
Glass seed beads (**NOTE:** Designer used dark mauve.)
¾ yd. **each** ⅛"-wide silk ribbon in two complementary colors (**NOTE:** Designer used dark mauve and medium green.)
Small scraps assorted colors felt
Mercerized sewing thread to match glove
Fine-line permanent-ink marking pen
Beading needle

1. Cut kid glove open alongside hand seam. Set aside.
2. Pin boot pattern right-side up atop felt. Trace around pattern. Remove pattern, flip, and pin wrong-side up atop felt. Trace around pattern. Remove pattern and cut out felt shapes. Set aside.

3. Place toe, heel, and tongue patterns right-side up atop kid leather. Trace around patterns and cut out. Cut one 1½" x ½" piece from kid leather for sentiment patch on back of boot. Set aside.

4. Pin boot pattern right-side up atop lining fabric. Trace around pattern. Remove pattern, flip, and pin wrong-side up atop fabric. Trace around pattern. Remove pattern and cut out fabric shapes, leaving a ¼" seam allowance around edges. Set aside.

5. Attach kid-leather toe, heel, and tongue to felt boot front along outside edges, using buttonhole stitch and sewing thread and referring to photo on page 126 for placement. Place a small amount of polyester filling under each kid-leather piece and blind stitch inside edge of each piece to boot front.

6. Work embroidery on boot front, using three strands of floss and referring to photo for color placement. The laces, as well as the creases on the toe and heel, are worked in straight stitch; the edge of the tongue is worked in outline stitch; and French knots are worked along the edge of the tongue.

7. Attach beads as desired, referring to photo for placement.

8. Write desired sentiment on right side of 1½" x ½" piece of kid leather. Whipstitch sentiment patch to back of boot, using green floss. Cut small circles from scraps of felt and attach to back of boot near sentiment patch, using yellow floss and French knots and arranging in a floral pattern. Refer to back schematic for placement. Work lazy-daisy leaves randomly, using green floss, to complete the pattern.

9. Turn under seam allowance on lining pieces, mitering corners, and press. Whipstitch to inside of boot front and back pieces, using sewing thread.

10. Holding front and back boot pieces together with right sides out, work button-hole stitch around boot to join pieces, using sewing thread. Place a small amount of polyester filling in toe of boot before sewing front and back pieces together in this area.

11. Tack silk-ribbon rosette to top, left corner of boot front.

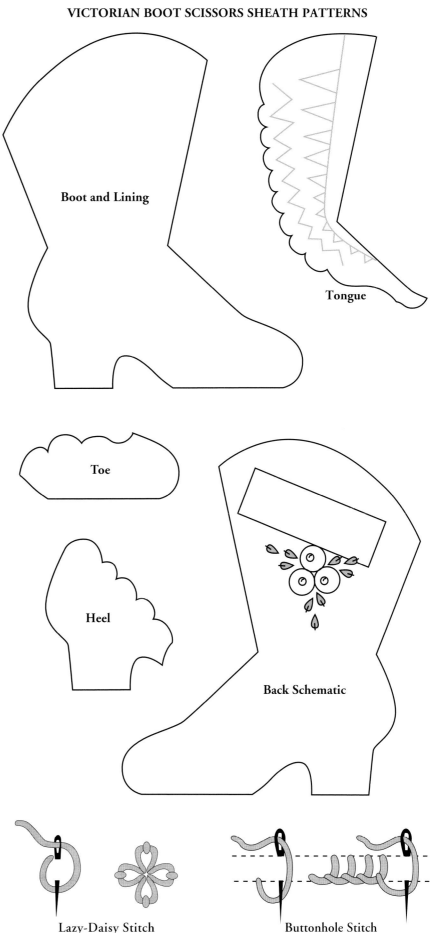

VICTORIAN BOOT SCISSORS SHEATH PATTERNS

Boot and Lining

Tongue

Toe

Heel

Back Schematic

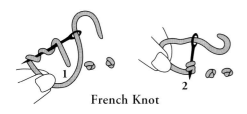

French Knot

Lazy-Daisy Stitch

Buttonhole Stitch

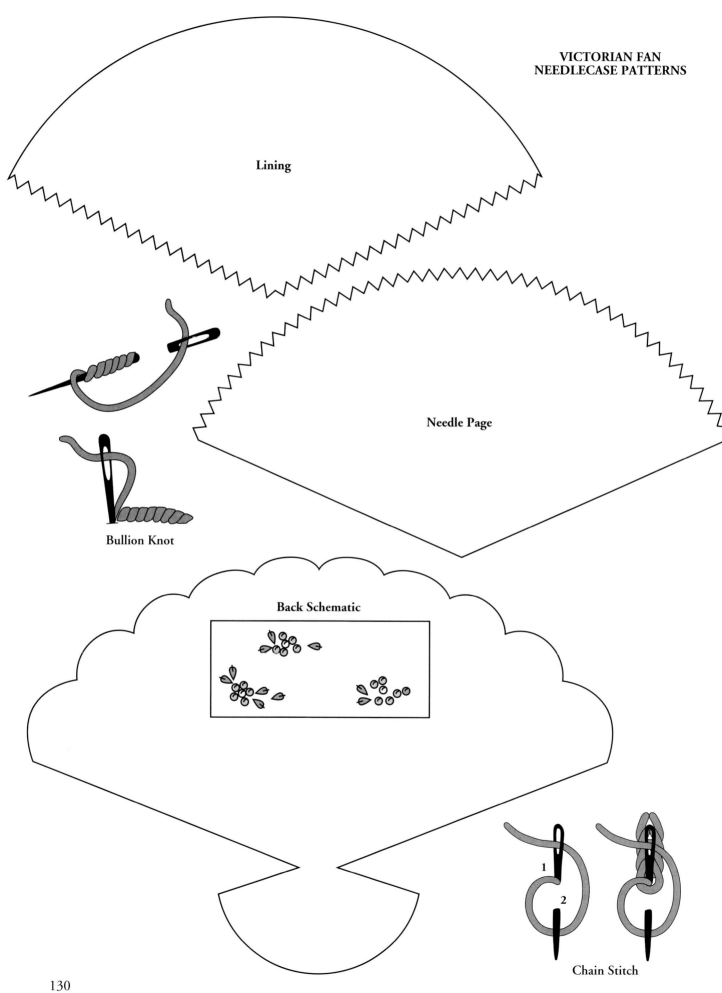

VICTORIAN FAN
NEEDLECASE PATTERNS

Lining

Needle Page

Bullion Knot

Back Schematic

1
2

Chain Stitch

130

Victorian Canoe Pincushion

Materials:

Vintage kid glove

7" x 5" piece print fabric to match felt hat (for pincushion)

Embroidery floss (**NOTE:** Designer used dark green, medium green, dark pink, light pink, and pale yellow.)

1½" yds. ¼"-wide light green silk ribbon, cut into two equal lengths

Crewel-embroidery needle

1. Cut kid glove open alongside hand seam. Set aside.

2. Pin canoe floor pattern right-side up atop felt. Trace around pattern. Remove pattern. Pin canoe side pattern right-side up atop felt. Trace around pattern. Remove pattern, flip, and pin wrong-side up atop felt. Trace around pattern. Remove pattern and cut out felt shapes. Set aside.

3. Place canoe gunnel pattern right-side up atop kid leather. Trace around pattern. Remove pattern, flip, and place wrong-side up atop leather. Trace around pattern. Remove pattern and cut out leather shapes.

4. Attach gunnels to upper edge of canoe front and back, using buttonhole stitch and two strands of embroidery floss to match felt. Stretch a small amount of polyester filling inside the gunnels. Whip-stitch lower edge of gunnels to felt.

5. Work embroidery on front and back of canoe, referring to pattern for color placement. Work French knots for center of each rose and as buds, using six strands of floss. Work bullion knots for roses, using six strands of floss. Work lazy-daisy stitch for leaves, using three strands of floss.

6. Holding canoe side pieces together with right sides out, work buttonhole stitch from Point A to Point B on one side, using sewing thread to match felt. Repeat for opposite side.

7. Place canoe floor within the sides, aligning evenly at bottom of canoe, and secure floor to sides, using a small running stitch and sewing thread to match felt.

8. To make pincushion, place polyester filling lengthwise in center of pincushion fabric. Shape to fit inside canoe firmly. Baste filling to fabric. Place assembled pincushion in opening at top of canoe. Baste in place to secure.

9. Tack silk-ribbon rosettes at each end of pincushion.

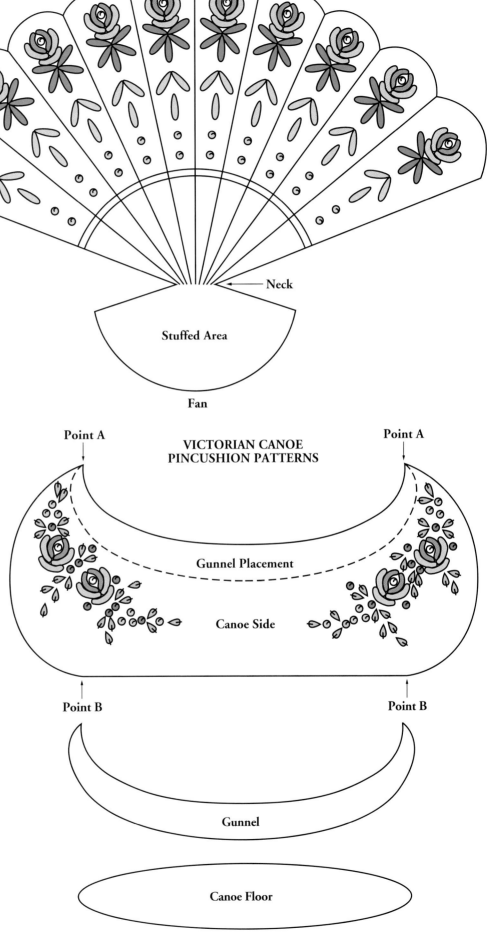

VICTORIAN CANOE PINCUSHION PATTERNS

Neck

Stuffed Area

Fan

Point A

Point A

Gunnel Placement

Canoe Side

Point B

Point B

Gunnel

Canoe Floor

Patrick's Sampler

While at first glance this sampler's size might indicate fairly simple stitchery, this diminutive design contains a treasury of stitches and techniques. This magnificent miniature, which features double running, Montenegrin, rice, Algerian eye, satin, queen, and chain stitches, as well as double backstitch variation and alternating double backstitch, will be a challenging yet pleasurable piece to complete.

*I*ncluding an assortment of added stitches, this tiny treasure will make a splendid addition to the sampler enthusiast's collection. It has the added benefit of displaying the needleworker's skills in a pleasing manner, without requiring an abundance of time to complete.

Patrick's Sampler

Kreinik

S	Soie d'Alger	DMC	DMC FT	
S	1736	930	2930	antique blue, dk.
C	2912	754	2754	peach flesh, lt.
∧	2916	347	2327	salmon, dk.
●	2231	3047	2579	yellow-beige, lt.
○	1835	367	2320	pistachio, dk.
+	1836	890	2890	pistachio, ul. dk.
X	1735	931	2931	antique blue, med.

Kreinik Metallics
#8 Fine Braid   gold

Fabric: 36-count summer khaki Edinborough linen from Wichelt Imports, Inc.
Stitch count: 136H x 90W
Design size:

25-count	10⅞" x 7¼"
28-count	9¾" x 6½"
32-count	8½" x 5⅝"
36-count	7½" x 5"

Instructions: Cross stitch over two threads, using one strand of silk.

Special instructions:
Areas 1 & 14: Work double backstitch variation using one strand of silk.
Area 2: Work Montenegrin stitch using one strand of silk.
Area 3: Work double running stitch using one strand 1735/931/2931.
Areas 4, 6, 11, & 13: Work alternating double backstitch using one strand of silk.
Area 5: Work double running stitch for flowers' edges, using one strand 2916/347/2327. Work rice stitch over two threads for center of each flower, using one strand of silk. Work Algerian eye stitch in boxed areas, using one strand of silk.
Area 7: Work satin stitch using one strand 1835/367/2320, stitching in direction indicated by arrows on Illustration 2.
Areas 8 & 10: Work double backstitch using one strand of silk.
Area 9: Work double running stitch for vines and flower outlines, using one strand 1736/930/2930 for stitches marked with uppercase letters, one strand 2916/347/2327 for stitches marked with lowercase let-

ters, and one strand 1836/890/2890 for stitches marked with numerals. Work satin stitch in flower centers, using one strand 2916/347/2327 on outside and one strand 2231/3047/2579 for centers. Work queen stitch in center of large flowers and for small flowers, using one strand of silk.
NOTE: Work first section of *Area 9* following Illustration 3. Work first vertical column following Illustration 4. Stitches C and B on Illustration 4 are the same as the solid black stitches on Illustration 3. Turn fabric 180° to work second section. Work second vertical column following Illustration 4. Turn fabric 180° again to work final section.
Area 12: Work double running stitch using one strand 1736/930/2930 for stitches marked with numerals and lowercase letters, and one strand 2916/347/2327 for stitches marked with uppercase letters. Work satin stitch for flower petals, using one strand 1735/931/2931. Work chain stitch between double-running-stitch borders of flowers, using one strand gold fine braid.

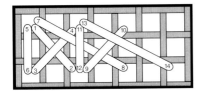

Double Backstitch Variation

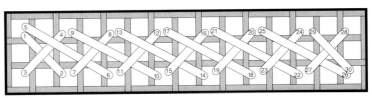

Double Backstitch

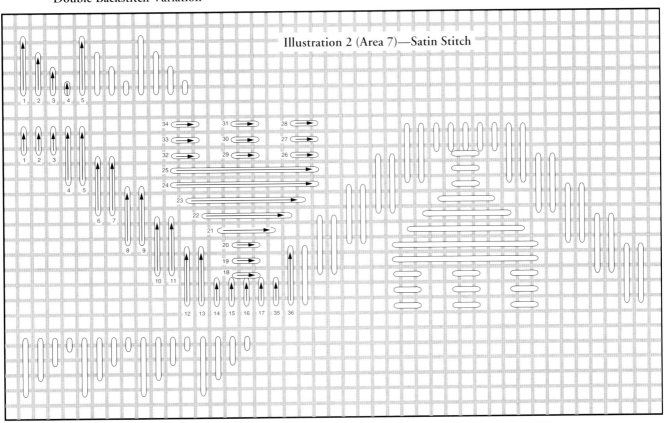

Illustration 2 (Area 7)—Satin Stitch

PATRICK'S SAMPLER

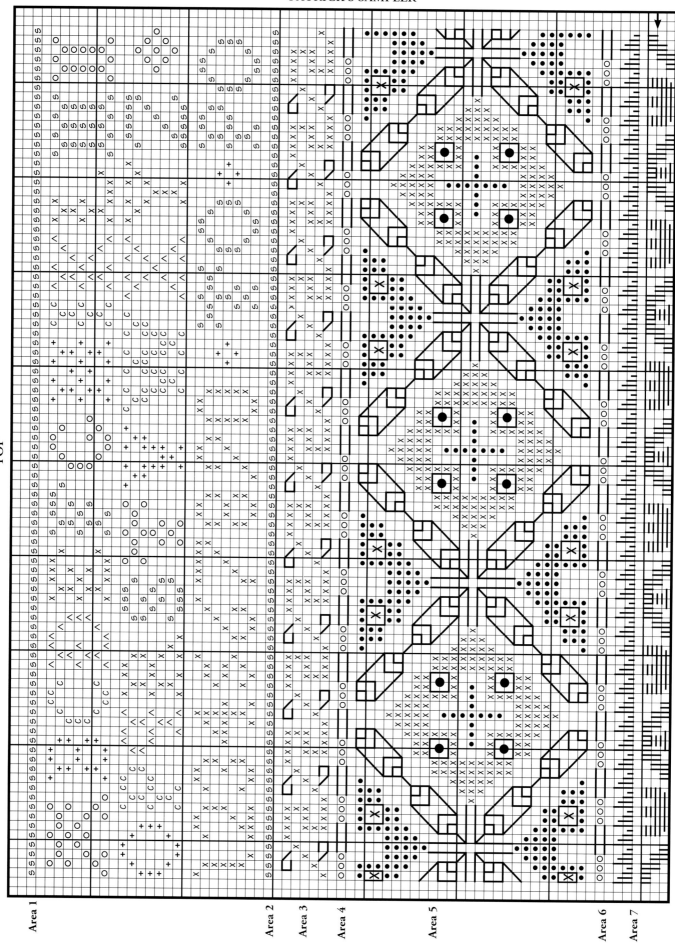

TOP

Area 1   Area 2   Area 3   Area 4   Area 5   Area 6 Area 7

134

Area 8   Area 9   Area 10   Area 11   Area 12   Area 13   Area 14

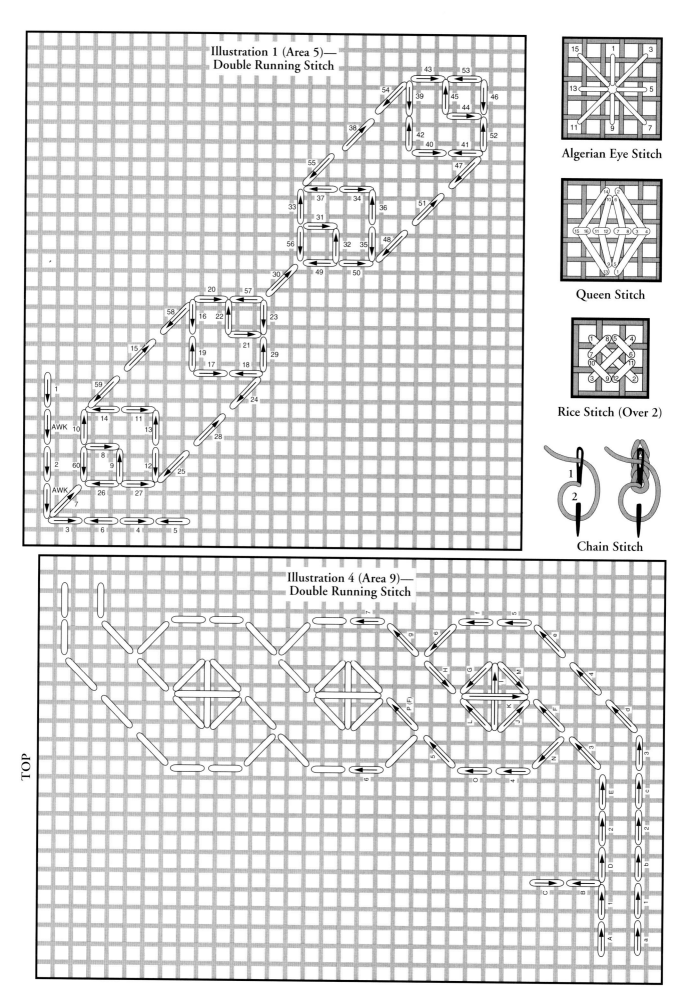

Illustration 1 (Area 5)—
Double Running Stitch

Algerian Eye Stitch

Queen Stitch

Rice Stitch (Over 2)

Chain Stitch

Illustration 4 (Area 9)—
Double Running Stitch

TOP

136

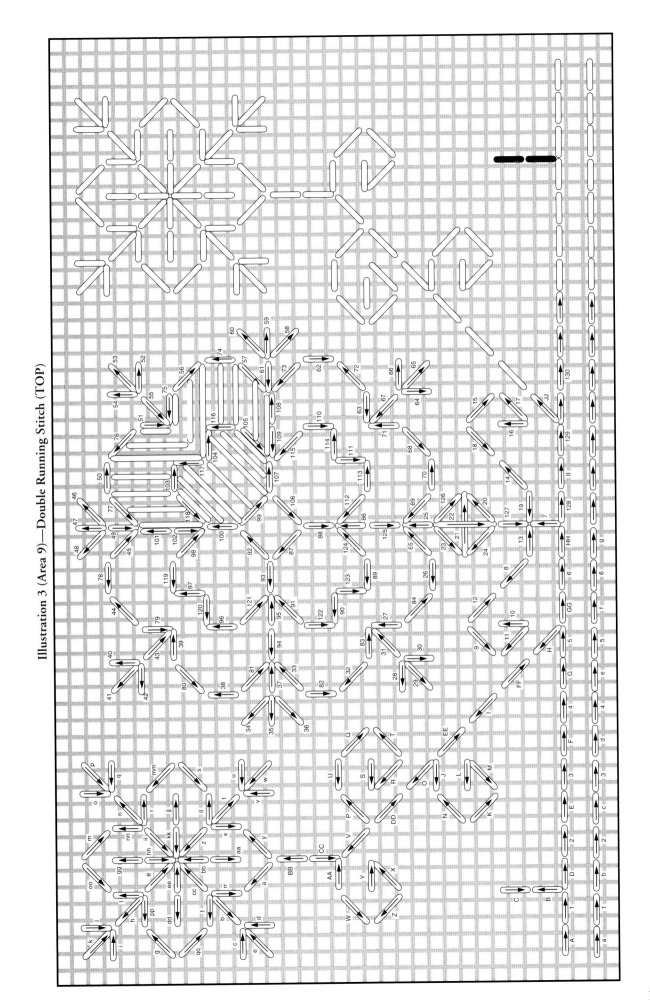

Illustration 3 (Area 9)—Double Running Stitch (TOP)

137

Illustration 5 (Area 12)—Double Running Stitch (TOP)

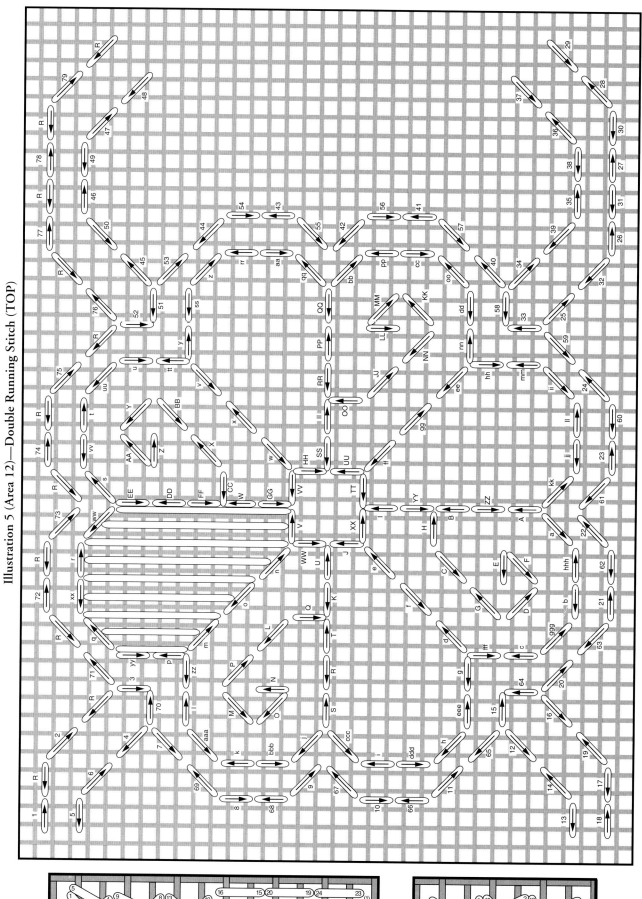

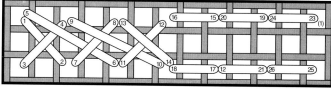

Alternating Double Backstitch

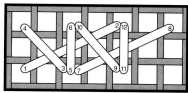

Montenegrin Stitch

Peacock Sampler

Designed to fit atop a needle-case with a magnetic interior, this vivid piece combines variegated cotton fibers and cotton embroidery floss in a design that was inspired by samplers of the past. This challenging miniature features cross stitch worked over one thread, and a variety of added stitches worked over two threads. Although the overall color scheme will be the same, each stitcher's creation will be unique, due to the nature of the variegated fibers.

Encompassing a variety of sampler stitches, this diminutive treasure contains a peacock motif from the Ann Bampton Sampler, *dated 1823.*

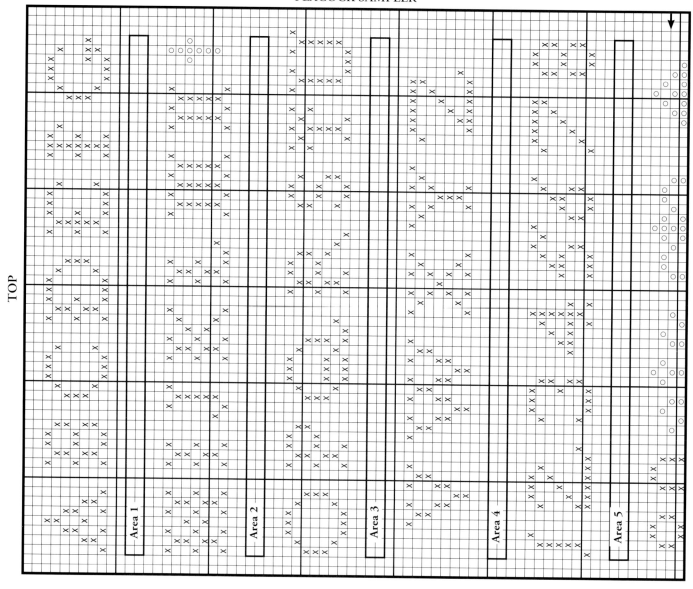

Peacock Sampler

		Kreinik	
	DMC	Soie	
DMC	FT	d'Alger	
○ 326	2326	1026	rose, vy. dp.
● 310	2310	noir	black
+ 644	2644	3831	beige-gray, med.
X 924	2924	206	gray-green,
			vy. dk.

The Caron Collection Wildflowers

╱ peacock
▲ pine forest
nefertiti

Fabric: 35-count unbleached linen from Norden Crafts

Stitch count: 134H x 55W
Design size:

28-count	4¾" x 2"
30-count	4½" x 1⅞"
32-count	4⅛" x 1¾"
35-count	3⅞" x 1½"

Instructions: Cross stitch over one thread, using one strand of floss.
NOTE: On this chart, one square equals one thread.

Special instructions:
Area 1: Work four-sided stitch over two threads, using one strand nefertiti.
Area 2: Work long-armed cross stitch over two threads, using one strand nefertiti.
Area 3: Work rice stitch over two threads, using one strand nefertiti.

Area 4: Work Smyrna cross stitch over two threads, using one strand nefertiti.
Area 5: Work eyelet stitch over two threads, using one strand nefertiti.
Area 6: Work satin stitch over four threads, using one strand nefertiti and working in direction indicated by lines on chart.
Area 7: Work queen stitch over four threads, using one strand nefertiti.

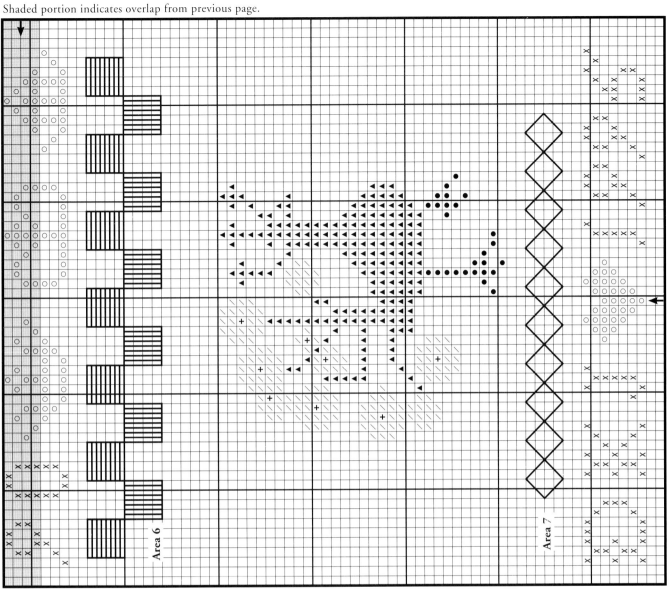

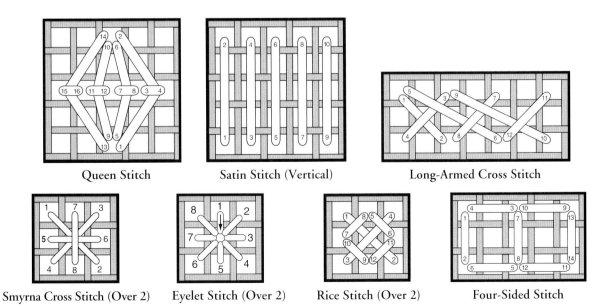

Queen Stitch   Satin Stitch (Vertical)   Long-Armed Cross Stitch

Smyrna Cross Stitch (Over 2)   Eyelet Stitch (Over 2)   Rice Stitch (Over 2)   Four-Sided Stitch

SOURCES FOR SUPPLIES

Pages 6-7, 88-89, & 112-113
Selected laces and linens from Attic Antiques, 5620 Cahaba Valley Road, Birmingham, AL 35242.

Noble-Dog Sampler
Page 18—Stitching paper available from Rose Cottage, 209 Richmond Street, El Segundo, CA 90245, (310) 322-8225. Louis XIV armoire and leather armchair, and ceramic and brass English whippet figurines from Carriage Antique Mall, 88 Greensprings Highway, Birmingham, AL 35209.

Harriet Hamlet Sampler
Page 24—Tea set from Attic Antiques. Pattern is *Filesia*. Frames from David's Arts & Frames, Inc., 3150 Cahaba Heights Village, Birmingham, AL 35243.

Tudor-Rose Sampler
Page 38—Coverlet and walnut, Victorian bed from Carriage Antique Mall.

Joshua and Caleb Sampler
Page 48—Reproduction candle screen available from Creative Furnishings, 12357 Saraglen Drive, Saratoga, CA 95070, (408) 996-7745. Candlesticks, books, and eighteenth-century armoire from Carriage Antique Mall.

Chatelaines: Traveling Companions of an Intimate Persuasion
Page 54—Selected antique chatelaines from Anne Powell, Ltd. [For a catalog of the company's offerings, send $5.00 to Anne Powell, Ltd., Post Office Box 3060, Stuart, FL 34995, (407) 287-3007]; selected antique chatelaines from Needlework Patio, Dallas, Texas, (214) 363-0351.

Late-Twentieth-Century Huswif
Page 64—Custom-dyed worsted-wool binding available from Textile Reproductions. [For a listing of the company's offerings, send $4.00 to Textile Reproductions, Box 48, West Chesterfield, MA 01084, (413) 296-4437.] Please specify project when ordering.

The Promise & Twisted-Ribbon Samplers
Page 120—Nineteenth-century modified whale-oil lamp and antique safeboxes from Attic Antiques.

Patrick's Sampler
Page 132—English half-moon buffet, silver tea server, and hand-painted ceramic platter from Carriage Antique Mall.

Peacock Sampler
Page 139—Dark cherry, wooden needlecase available from DJV Designs, Post Office Box 1075, Murrieta, CA 92564, 1-800-354-8474. Wooden workbox from Attic Antiques.

Custom framing by David's Arts & Frames, Inc., 3150 Cahaba Heights Village, Birmingham, AL 35243, (205) 967-0480.

Items not included in "Sources for Supplies" are either commonly available, antiques, or from private collections. Antiques included in "Sources for Supplies" were available from the merchants listed at the time photography was completed. Availability may vary depending on each merchant's sales since that time.

Artists and Artisans

Stitches in Time

Harriet Hamlet Sampler
Page 24, reproduced by Catherine G. Scott, stitched by Kayla Connors and Bettye Dwyer

Noble-Dog Sampler
Page 18, reproduced by Darlene O'Steen, stitched by Diane Kennedy-Jackson

Sarah Laker Sampler
Page 8, reproduced by Catherine G. Scott, stitched by April Taylor

Sarah Turner Sampler
Page 34, reproduced by Catherine G. Scott, stitched by Kayla Connors

Treasures for Tomorrow

Joshua and Caleb Sampler
Page 48, designed by Marie Barber, stitched by Kayla Connors

Guide My Heart Sampler
Page 80, designed by Marie Barber, stitched by Danielle Langner

Late-Twentieth-Century Huswif
Page 64, designed and stitched by Darlene O'Steen

Tudor-Rose Sampler
Page 38, designed by Angela Pullen, stitched by Catherine G. Scott

Elegance in White

Five-Band Sampler
Page 100, designed and stitched by Catherine G. Scott

Whitework Duet
Page 90, designed and stitched by Catherine G. Scott

Diminutive Works

The Promise Sampler
Page 120, designed and stitched by Anna I. Jackson

Patrick's Sampler
Page 132, designed by Darlene O'Steen, stitched by April Taylor

Peacock Sampler
Page 139, designed by Diane Kennedy-Jackson, stitched by April Taylor

Rose-Wreath Chatelaine
Page 114, designed and stitched by Merry Cox

Twisted-Ribbon Sampler
Page 120, designed and stitched by Anna I. Jackson

Victorian Treasures
Page 126, designed and crafted by Judith L. Knopp

Computer Charting

Rebecca Mitchell, Chris O'Steen, Mitzi Reeves

Custom Finishing

Claudia B. Wood

Acknowledgements

The editors gratefully acknowledge the generosity of the following companies and individuals who have provided materials for the production of the models and for the props and locations used in photographing them.

Attic Antiques

Carriage Antique Mall

The Caron Collection

Charles Craft, Inc.

Ashley C. Cobb

The DMC Corporation

Mr. and Mrs. Wayne Hoffman

Rose Marie King

Judith L. Knopp

Kreinik Manufacturing

Norden Crafts

Potpourri, Etc.

Textile Reproductions

Wichelt Imports, Inc.

Zweigart®

Index

Numbers in **bold** type indicate color-photo pages. All other numbers refer to pages for charts, color codes, patterns, and instructions.